THE ADMIRALTY

THE ADMIRALTY

by

N. A. M. RODGER, D.Phil., M.A.

★ ★ ★ ★ ★ ★ ★ ★ ★

Offices of State

Series Editor: M. M. Reese

★ ★ ★ ★ ★ ★ ★ ★ ★

TERENCE DALTON LIMITED

LAVENHAM SUFFOLK

1979

Published by
TERENCE DALTON LIMITED
ISBN 0 900963 94 8

Text photoset in 11/13pt Baskerville

Printed in Great Britain at
THE LAVENHAM PRESS LIMITED
LAVENHAM . SUFFOLK

Contents

Other Books in this Series

THE SECRETARY OF STATE

David Kynaston

THE LORD CHANCELLOR

Nicholas Underhill

Index of Illustrations

General Introduction

THE welcome given to the first two books in this series, on the Lord Chancellor and the Secretary of State, would seem to have recognised the need for a concentrated and cogent account of major British institutions. The vast learning made available in specialist studies has not, so far, been easily accessible in a simple and compact form to attract students and general readers interested in the origins and evolution of the principal instruments of government.

British institutions have been moulded by men and circumstances rather than dogmatic theory, and where great offices have suddenly taken long strides or moved in new directions, this has usually been due to particular national crises or to statesmen of outstanding calibre and determination. Thus the books in this series on the Offices of State aim to relate a general account of constitutional development to the quirks and achievements of the men who have occupied those offices. This brings a personal flavour to the narrative and reminds us that constitutional progress has seldom been achieved without passion and struggle.

Passion and struggle have never been absent from the history of "Their Lordships". Dr Rodger has published several articles on naval matters, and this book is the first attempt ever made to describe the evolution of the Admiralty within a tidy historical compass. The research is wide and the comment stimulating. It proves to be a remarkable story that may surprise readers taught to believe in the impregnability of British naval endeavour.

M. M. Reese,
Hindhead,
June 1979

Preface

"Memoirs are true and useful stars, whilst studied histories are the stars joined in constellations, according to the fancy of the poet."
Samuel Pepys [1]

OF ALL the responsibilities of government, few can be more troublesome than national defence. Armies, and still more navies, have always been large and complex organizations, vital to the safety of the state, but expensive and difficult to control. Before the twentieth century, no British government ever undertook a more onerous task than providing a fleet, or faced in a more acute form the problems of administration on a large scale. In early modern Europe, navies were the largest, the costliest and technically the most advanced organizations of their day; the hazards of putting a fleet to sea in the sixteenth century were equivalent to those of putting a man on the moon in the twentieth.

There is, moreover, a peculiar difficulty that affects all fighting services: they do not spend enough time fighting. During long periods of peace an organization has to be maintained perpetually prepared for war, but never allowed to practise it. The fighting man must spend his career making ready for a war which he may never have experienced, and may never experience. The administrator must run as efficiently and economically as possible a system which is always liable to be subjected without warning to sudden, violent and unpredictable strains.

It is not surprising, therefore, that the administration and direction of the Navy have for centuries faced the government of the country with its most intractable problems, and its attempts to solve them shed a most interesting light on social, administrative and political history. It is all the more surprising that the Admiralty has never attracted its biographer. Neither its modern constitution nor its ancient history has ever been fully treated. Yet the Admiralty was not the least of the departments of state; older, larger, with responsibilities unique in kind and scope, it stood out from other ministries not only because it was different, but because it felt itself to be different. Proud and often idiosyncratic, confident in itself and conscious of its long history, the

Admiralty was always unlike the rest. It carried into the late twentieth century a system of government designed in the early seventeenth, and yet it was arguably the most efficient of all ministries. The Royal Navy has not lacked historians, and yet the Admiralty, from which the Service's history can scarcely be disentangled, has been almost ignored, There need be no apology, therefore, for any attempt to fill the gap.

One of the problems facing any historian of the Admiralty is that it is not one but several subjects, reflected by the several meanings of the word. In its primary sense it refers to a general and ill-defined authority over sea affairs, or more exactly to the authority, office and jurisdiction of the Lord Admiral of England. In this sense "Admiralty" is almost the essence of naval history. When the office of Lord Admiral was put into commission, the Lords Commissioners for executing the office of Lord Admiral naturally became known as the Board of Admiralty, or simply as the Admiralty, and when in time they developed an administrative apparatus which grew to be the great ministry of modern times, the word acquired another sense again. The history of the Admiralty, as a department of state, can scarcely be brought back to the seventeenth century, but there were Lords Commissioners of various sorts—that is to say the office of Lord Admiral was in commission or abeyance—from 1628 to 1638, from 1642 to 1643, again from 1645 to 1648 and 1649 to 1660, from 1673 to 1684, from 1689 to 1702, from 1709 to 1827, and finally from 1828 to 1964. If the history of the Admiralty is equivalent to the history of the Board, it is both longer and much more disjointed than the history of the department. Moreover it cannot really be understood apart from the history of the Lords Admiral and their office. This book has therefore to deal with three distinct meanings of the word Admiralty. It must cast back some hundreds of years before the first Board of Admiralty received their patent or the first clerks took up their posts, and it might legitimately continue after the last Board had surrendered theirs, were it not prudent for the historian, writing only fourteen years later, to take heed of Sir Walter Raleigh's warning that "whosoever in writing a modern history, shall follow truth near the heels, it shall haply strike out his teeth". Throughout, the book has to do both with the political history of the Board and the administrative history of the Office; subjects too close to be separated, and yet distinct.

I have had to cover within a limited compass a great deal of material spread over a long period. Of necessity the reader is assumed to have a basic knowledge of English history, for the book is scarcely long enough to supply it if he has not. The constitutional history of naval administration in general, and the Admiralty in particular, has been covered completely, if not always in much depth, in order that this first study should at least serve as a text-book until supplemented by a fuller one, but I have tried to introduce some leaven of anecdote to lighten the administrative detail.

The notes and bibliography have been cast with the general reader in mind as well as the specialist. I have tried to refer to printed sources rather than documents, even when I had consulted the latter, considering that an adequate treatment in print would be more accessible to most readers than the documents themselves. The notes are contracted so far as is consistent with clarity, and a list of the abbreviations is prefaced to the bibliography, in which will be found the full titles of all works referred to in the notes by short title.

In writing the book I have been helped by numerous kindnesses, especially from my colleagues in the Public Record Office, among whom Dr E. M. Hallam and Dr J. B. Post were kind enough to read the manuscript, correct a few of its errors and ameliorate its style, and from my long-suffering friends Anne and Joachim Hettich, in whose house the book was written. Dr John B. Hattendorf generously gave me the benefit of his knowledge of naval administration during the War of the Spanish Succession. Mr E. K. Timings, now retired from the Public Record Office, gave me much encouragement and assistance during the early stages of the work. For myself I can only hope to have heeded in some measure the warning of Sir Thomas Browne:

> "Surely there goes a great deale of conscience to the compiling of an History; there is no reproach to the scandall of a Story; it is such an Authenticke kind of falsehood that with authority belies our good names to all Nations and Posteritie."[2]

N. A. M. Rodger
Chiswick,
Christmas 1978

[1]Tanner, *Pepys's Naval Minutes* [*PNM*], 69.
[2]*Religio Medici* Pt. II, Sect. iii.

CHAPTER ONE

LORDS ADMIRAL 1485-1628

21st September 1485-10th March 1513	John de Vere, Earl of Oxford
17th March 1513-25th April 1513	Sir Edward Howard*
4th May 1513-16th July 1525	Thomas, Lord Howard, later Earl of Surrey and Duke of Norfolk
16th July 1525-22nd July 1536	Henry Fitzroy, Duke of Richmond
16th August 1536-28th July 1540	William Fitzwilliam, Earl of Southampton
28th July 1540-December 1542	John, Lord Russell
December 1542-26th January 1543	Edward Seymour, Earl of Hertford
26th January 1543-17th February 1547	John Dudley, Viscount Lisle
17th February 1547-March 1549	Thomas, Lord Seymour
28th October 1549-14th May 1550	John Dudley, Earl of Warwick†
14th May 1550-October 1553	Edward, Lord Clinton
20th March 1554-10th February 1558	William, Lord Howard of Effingham
10th February 1558-16th January 1585	William, Lord Clinton, later Earl of Lincoln
8th July 1585-28th January 1619	Charles, Lord Howard of Effingham, later Earl of Nottingham
28th January 1619-23rd August 1628	George Villiers, Marquess, later Duke of Buckingham

COMMISSIONS OF ADMIRALTY 1628-1638

Senior Commissioners:

20th September 1628	Richard, Lord Weston, later Earl of Portland, Lord Treasurer
10th April 1635	Robert Bertie, Earl of Lindsey, Lord Great Chamberlain
16th March 1636	William Juxon, Bishop of London, Lord Treasurer

LORD ADMIRAL 1638-1642

13th April 1638	Algernon Percy, Earl of Northumberland

COMMISSION OF ADMIRALTY 1642-1643

Senior Commissioner:

19th October 1642	Algernon Percy, Earl of Northumberland

LORD ADMIRAL 1643-1645

7th December 1643	Robert Rich, Earl of Warwick

PARLIAMENTARY ADMIRALTY COMMITTEE 1645-1648

Senior Member:

19th April 1645	Algernon Percy, Earl of Northumberland**

*The last, and possibly the only Lord Admiral of England to be killed in action.

†See 1543-1547

**From December 1643 Francis, Lord Cottington, Charles I's Lord Treasurer, headed a commission of Admiralty from the King which remained nominally in force until the King's execution.

LORD ADMIRAL 1648-1649

29th May 1648- 23rd February 1649	Robert Rich, Earl of Warwick

COUNCIL OF STATE'S COMMITTEE ON THE ADMIRALTY AND NAVY 1649-1652

Senior Member:

12th March 1649	Sir Henry Vane jnr.

COMMITTEE ON ADMIRALTY AFFAIRS 1652-1653

Senior Member:

14th December 1652	Sir Henry Vane jnr.

ADMIRALTY COMMISSION 1653-1660

Senior Commissioners:

28th July 1653	General Robert Blake
22nd November 1655	Major-General John Lambert
24th December 1658	John, Lord Disbrowe
31st May 1659	Sir Henry Vane, jnr.
2nd February 1660	Robert Reynolds, Attorney-General

SECRETARIES TO LORDS ADMIRAL, ADMIRALTY COMMITTEES AND COMMISSIONS 1625-1660

1625-1638	Edward Nicholas
1638-1645	Thomas Smith
1645-1653	William Jessop and Robert Coytmore (jointly)§
1652-1660	Robert Blackburne

§Though superseded in December 1652, the Committee was not formally dissolved until the following year.

CHAPTER ONE

The Office of Admiralty

"For by wise counsel thou shalt make thy war: and in multitude of counsellors there is safety."

Proverbs XXIV, 6

THE office of Lord Admiral is of mediaeval origin. The word itself is Arabic, one of the many things brought from the Mediterranean world to the less civilized North. The first "Captains and Admirals" in England appear at the end of the thirteenth century. They were sea commanders, appointed for a particular campaign or expedition. Some of them may have had seafaring experience, but in most respects their position was no different from that of other middle-ranking military officers. They were generally knights, but not noblemen. None had any administrative responsibility for the King's ships.

The office (or offices, for there were often several admirals, of separate fleets) began to acquire a new importance in the fourteenth and fifteenth centuries with the development of civil law for maritime causes.[1] The growth of the Admiralty court gave to an Admiral a status and income which he had not enjoyed before. Though still fighting commanders at need, the various Admirals were becoming great officers of state. By the end of the fourteenth century it was rare for a mere knight to be an Admiral. Henry V took the dignity of the office a stage further by appointing an "Admiral of England", superior to all others, and after his death no more subordinate Admirals were created. The mediaeval Admiral, in his final and most familiar guise, was thus a product of the fifteenth century. He was a great officer of state, invariably a great nobleman. He derived a large income from his legal jurisdiction, and he was expected to command at sea when required, but he had no administrative responsibilities at all.[2]

Insofar as mediaeval Kings of England possessed a permanent administrator of their navies, he was the Clerk of the King's Ships.[3]

The post first appears in a distinct form under King John, when William de Wrotham was Keeper of the King's Ports and Galleys. Wrotham was evidently an able man, and he was entrusted with the management of the substantial fleets used during John's reign, applying to that purpose the receipts of his other office, Keeper of the Stannaries. But the office of Clerk of the King's Ships was not in reality any more permanent than the connection with tin mines, which did not survive Wrotham's death. An efficient Clerk, such as William Soper under Henry V, might be given charge of the raising of large fleets. A lesser man, under a king with no use for large fleets, might be left, like the ships themselves, to rot in a backwater:

> "The clerk of the ships was not a one-man department of state, but rather a permanent agent of the Crown, of little standing, available for the performance of certain duties which could as easily be entrusted to other hands, and often were."[4]

This remained under Henry VII as true as it had always been; in this as in other ways he was the last of the mediaeval kings. Robert Brigandine, Clerk of the Ships from 1495 to about 1523, had a large share in the cautious development of the Tudor navy. He built the first dry dock in England, and the new great ship *Henri Grace à Dieu.* But his predecessor, Thomas Roger, had been ignored, and shipbuilding entrusted to others. At the death of Henry VII in 1509 the Navy Royal was no nearer possessing a permanent administration than it had ever been.[5]

Henry VIII has traditionally, and in many ways justly, been regarded as the founder of the Royal Navy. If he was so, however, it was not so much because he increased his fleet tenfold, nor because he first mounted heavy guns in warships. Some mediaeval kings of England had had fleets, and even ships, as large. Henry's more lasting achievement was to provide the Navy with its first permanent administration, and thus to provide it, for the first time, with the means of a permanent existence.[6]

As the size of the Navy increased in the early years of the century, so it acquired shore establishments to support the ships. The first dock, which Brigandine had built in 1496, was at Portsmouth, but most of the nascent dockyards were on or near the Thames. In 1514 John

Hopton was appointed "Keeper of the Storehouses" at Erith, Deptford and Portsmouth. The name suggests that he was, in origin, quite a humble official, but within a few years he was taking a central part in naval administration. He and his successor, William Gonson, became in effect paymasters of the Navy. Early in the reign so simple an operation as the shifting of the *Gabriel Royal* from Barking Creek to Woolwich required a whole series of writs and warrants specifically authorizing various officers to do their parts; before many years were out Hopton, and later Gonson, were being trusted with lump sums to spend on naval administration as they thought fit. In March 1539 Gonson was paid £500 "to be by him employed abowte his highnes affaires upon the See". During the war of 1542 to 1546 this became a general practice. The "Clerk Comptroller" was reduced to an assistant, or at least a junior colleague, of Gonson.

The increasing business of the war led in 1544 to the installation of William Broke as Surveyor of the King's Ships. There were now three officials with large but ill-defined responsibilities for the administration of the Navy. Gonson, by virtue of his financial control, was effectively the most important, but there was no formal unity of action, and no regular channel of communication with the Lord Admiral or the captains of the ships.[7]

In 1545 Gonson committed suicide, and thus perhaps hastened a process of reform which was probably already under way. The details remain shadowy, and it is hard to be sure who was responsible for the changes, and what exactly it was hoped to achieve by them, but the nature of the new administration is clear. By letters patent of 20th April 1546, applied retrospectively from the previous Christmas, the Principal Officers of the Navy were increased in number, and formed into a body later to be known as the Navy Board, but at first called the "Council of the Marine", the "Chief Officers of the Admiralty", or simply "the Admiralty". Its members were seven: the Lieutenant of the Admiralty, the Treasurer of Marine Causes, the Comptroller, Surveyor and Clerk of the King's Ships, and two Assistants. To them was soon added a Master of the Ordnance for the King's Ships. The Lieutenant of the Admiralty was to preside at the Board as the Lord Admiral's deputy, and the Principal Officers were to be "the conduit pipes to whom the Lord Admiral properly directs all commands for his

Majesty's service and from whom it descends to all other inferior officers and ministers under them whatsoever". For the first time, a proper and permanent connection was provided between the political direction (the King and Council), the high command (the Lord Admiral), and the actual administration of the fleet.[8]

It is a matter of some controversy to what extent this new Board reflected the organizing genuis of Thomas Cromwell, and his drive for "conciliar government". It can have been influenced by him only indirectly, as he had been dead six years in 1546. There is no doubt, however, that the board was a form of government just then in fashion. The Navy Board closely followed the constitution of the Ordnance Board, especially in the position of the Lieutenant, corresponding to the Lieutenant of the Ordnance as deputy of the Master of the Ordnance.

The Board structure provided certain obvious benefits. It spread the load of an increased burden of administration without unduly fragmenting it. It provided some financial check on the Treasurer, (who was obliged to have his warrants countersigned by two of his colleagues), and a species of collective control on the actions of the other Principal Officers. It spread the risk inherent in trusting too much to one man, however honest and competent, and it offered the stability of continuity.

Administrative stability, however, was in the circumstances of the sixteenth century very limited. The political vicissitudes which followed Henry VIII's death brought change and decay to the Navy, and to the Navy Board. Nevertheless, there were solid achievements. During Edward VI's reign the anchorage at Gillingham, later Chatham Dockyard, was first used, and victualling of the fleet reorganized under a General Surveyor of Victuals for the Seas. In 1557 the Treasurer was accorded an "Ordinary"; that is, a regular annual sum to cover standing charges, and with it there were 320 shipwrights employed in the three dockyards of Deptford, Woolwich and Portsmouth.[9]

The Navy Board had now become one of the largest departments of the government, as well as one of the biggest industrial enterprises in the country. It had also acquired a rôle unmentioned in its patent. As a body of experienced naval administrators, the Board was the natural adviser on naval affairs of the Lord Admiral and the Council; the

Admirals usually, and the Council invariably being inexpert in them. In this the Navy Board was fulfilling one of the functions of the later Board of Admiralty. One of the papers presented to Queen Elizabeth on her accession was an estimate by the Board of the proper size and composition of her fleet; in effect, a naval standard. It is clear that by this date the Board was meeting regularly to consider the "weighty affairs" of the Navy.[10]

By this time, also, a very significant departure from the original structure of the Board had been made. The post of Lieutenant of the Admiralty had been allowed to lapse, leaving the Board without a chairman. In 1556 the Council directed the Lord Treasurer to assume control, with the advice of the Lord Admiral. In practice the Treasurer of the Navy presided at the Board, reporting to the Lord Treasurer, who thus secured from the Lord Admiral control of one of the largest and most expensive departments of state, and confined the Lord Admiral to his ancient functions.[11] William Paulet, marquess of Winchester, was then Lord Treasurer, and Benjamin Gonson (son of William) Treasurer of the Navy; both were able and honest men, under whose direction the Ordinary of the Navy was reduced from £14,000 per annum of 1557 to below £10,000 in 1560. The Navy was less expensive and possibly more efficient, but at the same time the Navy Board was more politically dependent, and hence open to corruption, as a result of the change. Moreover, the independence of naval administration was sharply curtailed, though in practice the system worked as well for the Navy and the country as the limitations of the age permitted, especially after Sir John Hawkins became Treasurer of the Navy in 1578.

By the year of the Armada, the Navy Royal had a developed and reasonably effective administration, by the standards of the time; but those standards were very different from ours. The possible achievements of even the best sixteenth-century administration were severely limited by the logistical problems of building, maintaining, arming, manning, and above all victualling a fleet at sea. Moreover the officials of the time looked on office and administration in a way profoundly unlike that of any modern functionary. Many of the members of the Navy Board were bitter personal enemies; some, like

Hawkins, had won their posts "by way of accusation" of their predecessors or colleagues.[12] Their loyalties outside themselves lay with the person of the Queen, not in any abstract idea of the Queen's service or the welfare of the Navy. Office, for them, was a piece of private property, to be exploited, honestly or dishonestly, for personal profit. The idea of forming part of a unified administrative machine came hardly to them; they each had an office, which might or might not involve the oversight of others, or the employment of private clerks to help them, but the modern concept of a government would scarcely have been understood by them:

> "The loyalty of sixteenth-century officials—apart, of course, from the most senior and responsible—was similar to that of private men. An official occupied a position of trust and emolument. He had been given that place either because he had earned it by past services; or because he had bought it; or because he had been lucky in securing the patronage of some great man. He was expected to perform certain duties, to transact certain pieces of business according to rules, if and when he was called upon to do so, either by the government, or by a private person, such as a petitioner or litigant. He received a separate fee for each job done. If he were a loyal conscientious official he would do what he was asked to do, protect the royal interest to the best of his ability, and refrain from oppression and fraud. On the other hand, he did not think himself as being in full-time employment, as being committed to the active and continuous service of the Crown and to the furtherance of its policies.[13]

The Lord Admiral, also, held office in a way which would be impossible to-day. He was in no modern sense a minister of the Crown; he was one of the great officers of state, whose positions and prestige derived from antiquity. His was an office of honour and profit; honour from commanding the Queen's forces in action, profit from the Court of Admiralty. The tendency to acquire administrative responsibility had been nipped in the bud by the Lord Treasurer's successful "take-over" of the Navy Board. In all essentials the Lord Admiral remained a mediaeval officer of state, and Charles, Lord Howard of Effingham, later earl of Nottingham, who was Lord Admiral from

1585 to 1619, was in many ways the last of the mediaeval Admirals. He was at his best commanding at sea—not that he had any sea experience, for that was not yet expected of a great nobleman, but he filled his natural and rightful place as the commander of the fleet, and received unquestioned obedience from his quarrelsome and undisciplined advisers. Most of the Navy Board were at sea in that fateful year of 1588, exercising, with others, their functions as advisers to the Admiral, and showing also that their duties as administrators still sat lightly on their shoulders.

Nottingham's essentially mediaeval view of his responsibilities showed to best effect in 1588, but in James's reign it led to disaster. Hawkins and Winchester were dead, and the new King had none of the shrewdness and parsimony of the old Queen. The times were unpropitious for financial honesty, and the energies of great men about the court were devoted to faction. So long as the Howard party, with Nottingham at its head, was in the ascendant, the affairs of his protégés were unlikely to be questioned. The Treasurer of the Navy was Sir Robert Mansell, appointed by Nottingham in 1604, and Sir John Trevor was Surveyor. Both were forceful and unscrupulous men, and the other Principal Officers could not touch them. Under Mansell and Trevor fraud was elevated to a level seldom matched in the long and extravagant history of corruption. In the case, Trevor and Mansell constructed a ship called the *Resistance,* in a dockyard, entirely with the King's materials and labour. Claiming her as their own, they chartered her to the King as a storeship. She was laden with the King's stores, but shortly parted company with the squadron and proceeded on a profitable voyage on her own account, selling the stores and freighting another cargo back to England.[14]

These "very great and intolerable abuses, deceits, frauds, corruptions, negligences, misdemeanours and offences" were scarcely concealed, but so long as the Howards remained in favour, their misdeeds remained unpunished. There was a small tremor in 1608, when a family quarrel weakened the Howard position, and as a result of the attacks of Nottingham's cousin the earl of Northampton, a Commission of Enquiry was appointed into naval administration. The report was pedestrian and verbose, but made it plain enough that the Navy was sinking into decay even as its expenses rose steeply. James received it blandly and did nothing.

It may seem incredible to modern readers that such corruption could be tolerated. Certainly, even then, a line was drawn between honest and dishonest profits from office. It was drawn with difficulty and hesitation, but contemporaries were in no doubt that Mansell and Trevor were abusing their trust. Their security of tenure—in an age when civil servants were almost as difficult to remove as now—derived from two circumstances in which the early Stuart administration faithfully followed its predecessors. All "civil servants", even the most junior, were in some sense political—that is, they derived their offices from personal contact, favours done and granted or pressure brought to bear. The idea of promotion on merit was almost unknown. So long as the conditions which had brought a man to office continued to operate, his tenure was safe, however well or ill he conducted himself. Even if his patrons died or lost favour, he was still secure in the enjoyment of what was unquestionably regarded as a piece of property. Offices were bought and sold, bargained, inherited, mortgaged and bequeathed like any other property. It was hardly easier to dismiss an official for misconduct that to dispossess a landowner for inefficiency in the management of his estates. At worst, a man might be compelled to sell or otherwise relinquish his office—suitably compensated, of course.[15]

The 1608 Commission of Enquiry failed because the circumstances were unpropitious for any attack on James's Howard favourites, or James's personal extravagance. Ten years later things were different. The possibility and even the attraction of economy had been demonstrated to the King by that energetic foe of corruption, Lionel Cranfield. More significantly, the fortunes of the Howards were waning as those of the young duke of Buckingham and his family waxed. Buckingham had a use for a stick to beat the Howards, and the power to wield it. A campaign for reform—that is, an attack on the corruption of Howard clients—could at last look to a powerful patron for support.[16]

In these circumstances the Privy Council, in the summer of 1618, set on foot a Royal Commission to enquire into naval administration. The arrangements it made are worth examining in detail because, although not unusual for the time, they were productive of significant changes in the management of the Navy.

Royal commissions were a typical instrument of early Stuart government, and might serve many purposes. Some, such as the Commission for the Advancement of the Fisheries, were standing commissions, hardly to be distinguished from the lesser Privy Council committees, and acted as official, or officially sponsored, agencies for the promotion of some beneficial trade or manufacture. Some, on the other hand, were a covert means to grant monopolies and other private favours, while others again were special enquiries, and some, like the Council of the North, had become permanent organs of administration. These commissions were very numerous, their membership often overlapped, and their functions became confused. They must have been a very inefficient means of achieving some ends, but they involved people of influence in the workings of government without the necessity of paying them salaries, and in the circumstances of the time it is hard to see how some such instrument could have been dispensed with.[17]

This Commission was a strong one, including men of ability, influence, and knowledge of naval affairs. Its terms of reference covered not only corruption and maladministration, but the future size and policy of the Navy, "the present institutions of the navy, and how it might be improved". Secure in Buckingham's favour, they did their work well. It would be impossible to better Cranfield's acid comments on what they found, "as that when ships were to be brought up to Woolwich or Deptford to be repaired, it had been better for his Majesty to have given them away at Chatham, and £300 or £400 in money, to any that would have taken them". He referred with satisfaction to their work in clearing the lists of non-existent ships left there to the profit of officials, "conjuring and driving away the spirits of ships long departed". By the end of the year Mansell had sold his office to a wealthy City merchant (Sir John Trevor was already dead), and Nottingham had been bought out by Buckingham himself.[18]

The significance of the Commission lay less in its successful onslaught on corruption than in its constitutional innovations. Like many an individual of the age, the Commission ended its catalogue of the faults of office-holders with an offer to take their place and do the work more cheaply and efficiently. Buckingham accepted the offer. For the next ten years, therefore, the Navy Board was suspended, and a standing commission, under the Lord Admiral, governed the navy. Only the Treasurer of the Navy remained as an independent official, but closely supervised by the Lord Treasurer. The Lord Admiral was now the head of an effective naval administration, as Henry VIII had intended him to be. Looking at the Commission in another way, he was chairman of what was hardly to be distinguished from a committee of the Privy Council, forming the link between the practical administration of the Navy and the inner councils of state very much as later First Lords were to do. The new administrative system was reasonably successful. The magnitude of the expeditions of 1625 and 1626 overwhelmed it, but it must be doubtful if any early seventeenth-century naval adminstration could have coped with such a strain without adequate finance.[19]

A standing royal commission was in itself a commonplace, but one responsible to the Lord High Admiral* necessarily involved him in its duties. Whether or not Buckingham's only initial interest in the office had been a political one, he was by no means an ineffective or indifferent head of naval administration. In this he altered the position of the Lord Admiral; no longer just a great officer of state in the ancient mould, but something more like a responsible minister.[20]

Buckingham's assassination in 1628 therefore removed an officer whose peace-time functions had become more than merely honorific. He left a vacuum in the administration; he also left a young widow and enormous debts. It was the debts rather than the vacuum which prompted the formation of the first Board of Admiralty to take his place. Edward Nicholas, Buckingham's private secretary for Admiralty affairs, devised and presented to the King a scheme whereby the Admiral's purely naval functions should be put into commission, leaving the Judge of Admiralty independent, and reserving the profits to the King to pay off Buckingham's debts and provide for the duchess. Charles I was anxious to provide for his favourite's widow and the scheme was accepted. Thus, for temporary and purely financial reasons the post of Lord Admiral was first put into commission.[21]

It was not intended that the office should be altered in function by this change, but inevitably it was. The new Board's patent was the first to give expression to the developments of Buckingham's time by mentioning administrative responsibilties. Moreover it eliminated one

* Buckingham was the first to be styled "Lord High Admiral".

aspect of Buckingham's office which had remained very much in the pattern of earlier years. Buckingham had been a pluralist on a grand scale; he was not only Lord Admiral, but Master of the Horse, Lord Warden of the Cinque Ports, Chief Justice in Eyre South of the Trent, Gentleman of the Bedchamber and Chief Clerk of King's Bench – most of which offices he executed in person. Only to a limited extent could he be an effective head of all these bodies. Such pluralism was an accepted feature of seventeenth-century administration, and often a deliberate contrivance for administrative efficiency. Nicholas, for example, besides being Buckingham's Admiralty Secretary and later Secretary of the Admiralty Board from 1625 to 1638, was also Secretary of the Fisheries Commission from 1630 to 1640 and Clerk of the Privy Council from 1626 to 1641 – installed specifically to guide the Council in naval matters.[22]

In the long run, however, more efficient naval administration inevitably meant more specialization and less overlapping, and in this the new Board in effect showed the way. Its structure was that of an ordinary Privy Council committee, and the individual members had many other responsibilities, but as a collective body they represented nothing but the central direction of the Navy. Detailed administration was in the hands of the Navy Board, now reconstituted, which was responsible to the Admiralty Board.

In other ways too, the new system set the pattern for the future, even though it did not radically depart from existing precedents. The career of Edward Nicholas, who began as a private employee of Buckingham and became the first of a long line of influential Secretaries of the Admiralty Board, is itself a pointer to the future. It would be going too far to call him the type of a modern civil servant, owing an impersonal loyalty to the machinery of government, but he was a prototype of the Admiralty Secretaries of later ages in being the expert adviser, sometimes guide and mentor, of the Board.

The approach of civil war disrupted these arrangements. In 1638 the earl of Northumberland was appointed Lord Admiral, to conciliate the moderate Puritan faction to which he belonged. When Parliament secured control of the fleet, the dockyards and the naval administration, Northumberland acquiesced in its authority and was continued in his post. The earl of Warwick, already commander-in-chief at sea, succeeded him in 1643 and continued until the Self-Denying Ordinance obliged him to resign in 1645. The circumstances of civil war forced Parliament to give very large powers to the commander at sea, and exercise only a distant control by the Committee of the Navy and Customs, whose business was largely financial, and its inner committee, the Admiralty Committee, which was responsible for "the whole frame of the affairs of the Admiralty and Cinque Ports". From 1645 to 1648 this functioned as an Admiralty Board, with the same Secretary, Thomas Smith, who had previously served Northumberland. In 1648 the Scots invasion and mutiny in the fleet brought Warwick back as Lord Admiral for a year, with the Derby House Committee taking over the higher direction of naval affairs.[23]

Until 1648 Parliament exercised a control, not always very effective, by a series of committees. Perhaps, if Parliamentary rule had continued, this system might have matured into a stable administration, but Pride's Purge in December, and the effective installation of a military dictatorship, brought about another abrupt change. The Council of State now took the direction of naval affairs into its own hands. The Lord Admiral's office was abolished, and the Navy Board replaced by a Navy Commission, doing much the same work as before. The Council of State delegated naval affairs to its Admiralty Committee, but it was still a cumbersome arrangement, with much detailed and technical business coming before the full Council of State.

All this administrative expedient and experiment took place while the size of the Navy was increasing rapidly, and for the most part in time of war, throwing an enormous strain on the makeshift organization at the centre. It is true that the Commonwealth and Protectorate inherited a working system of practical administration, the Navy Board and its subordinate dockyards, which was improved and expanded but not essentially altered. Nevertheless, the concentration of all power in the Council of State was an impossible arrangement, and the defeat of Dungeness in 1652 finally forced the creation of a Committee on Admiralty Affairs. This in its turn was ejected with the Rump in April 1653, when an Admiralty Commission was installed, which continued to direct the Navy until the Restoration. The wheel had now turned full circle, with an Admiralty Board (in all but name) and a Navy Board (in all but name) just as before.[24]

The naval administration of the Commonwealth and Protectorate built up fleets of a size and efficiency undreamed of under Charles I, and made the English Navy master of the waters of Northern Europe, and even the Mediterranean, for the first time. It was unquestionably more effective than its Stuart predecessor, which had been unable properly to fit out and victual fleets to La Rochelle and the Île de Rhé twenty-five years before. The contrast is striking, and some historians have not hesitated to draw it in moral terms, comparing the corruption and degradation of the Stuarts with the honesty and firm purpose of Puritan rule. There is some truth in this view, but it has been crudely overdrawn. The truth, as Lady Bracknell tells us, is never pure and rarely simple; the career of the younger Sir Henry Vane may be taken to illustrate the strengths and shortcomings of the new men of the Interregnum.

Vane was a man of extraordinary ability and energy, a passionate supporter of the cause for which he fought, and a ruthless opponent of its enemies. As Treasurer of the Navy from 1639 (when he bought a half-share from Sir William Russell) until 1650, as the dominant figure on the Admiralty Board of 1645 to 1648 and the Admiralty Committees of the Council of State until 1653, his skill, determination and prodigious industry were more than anything else (save financial backing) responsible for the success and growth of the Navy. At the same time he possessed many of the characteristic vices of Stuart politicians. He made enormous sums from the Treasurership, freely ignoring Parliamentary resolutions to do so. Though not exactly dishonest, he was a man who thought himself, in Clarendon's phrase, "loosed from ordinances". He did not hesitate to put his politics before what might be regarded as the national interest. He stayed away from the Admiralty Committee during the summer of 1652, paralysing its work and threatening the safety of the country, because he disapproved of the Dutch War. His biographer speaks of his "duplicity", and of "a certain lack of honesty which marks much of his political career".[25]

Against this picture of Sir Henry Vane we may set others to exemplify the "Stuart" and "modern" aspects of republican rule. On the one hand stand the twenty-four captains investigated for fraud between 1652 and 1660, or the vast family business of the Petts, which waxed fat on corruption in the dockyards throughout the reigns of

James and Charles, and continued with profit and impunity under their successors. On the other are William Jessop, Robert Coytmore and Robert Blackburne, successive Secretaries of the Admiralty from 1645 to 1660, whom we may justly regard at the ancestors of the modern civil servant. Competent, industrious and non-political, they served the state whatever their private opinions about its form of government. Several had served Charles I and were to serve his son. In them we see the germ of the Admiralty as a permanent, professional, department of state.[26]

By 1660 the Admiralty in this sense was only an embryo. Though the Navy Board had now a continuous history of over a century, with a large permanent staff and great enterprises under its direction, the Admiralty remained no more than a tentative solution to the problem of providing central direction of the Navy. Under Charles I and Cromwell, it had been found to answer well to certain demands, but it was far from being an accepted form of government. Half a century was still to pass before the Board of Admiralty began to be accepted as the normal means of directing the Navy's affairs. But by 1660 certain traditions had already been established. The idea that boards or committees were, or could be, more stable authorities than individuals, and that they needed to be advised and served by efficient and impartial secretaries, had insensibly crept into public opinion. In these ideas lay the essence of the later Admiralty, and in the next half-century the ideas were to have a chance to develop.[27]

NOTES

1 Marcus, *Naval History* I, 15. Oppenheim, *History,* 2-5. Marsden, *Select Pleas* I, xlii.

2 Perrin, MM XII, 117. De Beer, MM XIII, 45. James and Shaw, BIHR XIV, 172.

3 Oppenheim, 3-4, 12-24, 32-35. Powell, EHR LXXI, 177.

4 Davies, EHR LXXX, 270.

5 Oppenheim, 32-36.

6 Davies, *passim.*

7 Davies, 274. Johns, MM XIV, 32.

8 Oppenheim, 84-86. Johns, 41. Davies, 272-274. Williamson, *Hawkins,* 319. Glasgow, MM LVI, 3-4. Oppenheim, *Monson's Tracts,* III, 398.

9 Davies, 276-278. Glasgow, 4-9.

10 Glasgow, 14-15.

11 Glasgow, 20. Murray, *Admiralty,* II, 140-141.

12 Williamson, 331.

13 Parry, *Age of Reconnaissance,* 370.

14 Aylmer, EHR LXXII, 232-234. McGowan, *Jacobean Commissions,* xiii-xv.

15 Aylmer, *King's Servants,* 10, 76, 102.

16 Prestwich, *Cranfield,* 211-216. Aylmer, EHR LXXII, 231-235. McGowan, xvii-xxviii. Murray, II, 140.

17 Aylmer, EHR LXXII, 232.

18 Prestwich, 212-215. McGowan, xix-xxviii.

19 Aylmer, EHR LXXII, 234-235.

20 James and Shaw, 11. Perrin, 129.

21 Murray, II, 143. James and Shaw, 172-176. Aylmer, EHR LXXII, 235. Perrin 129. Nicholas, *Secretary Nicholas,* 38-67.

22 Oppenheim, *History,* 279-282. Murray, II, 143-146. James and Shaw, 173-175. Aylmer, EHR LXXII, 235. Perrin, 129. Aylmer, *King's Servants,* 126, 132-133. Nicholas, 56.

23 Perrin, 132-134. Dewar, MM XII, 406-415. Murray, II, 143-145. Rowe, *Vane,* 94-95, 120-135. Aylmer, *King's Servants,* 360. Kennedy, MM XLVIII, 276-290. Kennedy, EHR LXXVII, 247. Oppenheim, *History,* 302-306.

24 Oppenheim, *History,* 313-361. Murray, II, 147. Gardiner, *First Dutch War,* I, 53-54. Dewar, 415-422. Rowe, 152-189. Aylmer, *State's Servants,* 14-18, 38-45.

25 Rowe, *passim,* especially 7-19, 58, 94-95, 128-131, 152-172, 181-189, 251-260. Aylmer, *State's Servants,* 15, 45.

26 *Idem,* 99, 156-160, 234-238, 265-266, 340.

27 Aylmer, *State's Servants,* 11, 38, 42, 156.

CHAPTER TWO

LORD ADMIRAL 1660-1673

29th January 1661*	James, Duke of York

COMMISSIONS OF ADMIRALTY 1673-1684

Senior Commissioners:

9th July 1673	Prince Rupert
14th May 1679	Sir Henry Capel
19th February 1681 -19th May 1684	Daniel Finch, later Earl of Nottingham

THE KING AS LORD ADMIRAL 1684-1688

19th May 1684	King Charles II
6th February 1685	King James II

SECRETARIES OF THE ADMIRALTY 1660-1688

July 1660	Sir William Coventry
September 1667	Matthew Wren
July 1672	Sir John Werden
June 1673	Samuel Pepys
May 1679	Thomas Hayter
February 1680	John Brisbane
May 1684	Samuel Pepys

*James acted as Lord Admiral from the Restoration.

CHAPTER TWO

A Secretary of the Marine

> "The life of a virtuous Officer in the Navy is a continual war defensive, viz: against the Ministers of State, and in particular the Lord Treasurers, in time of peace, and all prejudiced inquisitors and malcontents with the Navy management in time of war."
>
> Samuel Pepys[1]

ON 29th May 1660 King Charles II rode through the streets of London crowded with his rejoicing subjects. With him rode his brother James, duke of York, nominally Lord High Admiral of England since 1649.[2] The preceding twenty years had brought for the people war and usurpation, dictatorship and instability, and for the King and the Duke, peril and exile. The cheering crowds looked to their king to restore order and tranquillity. There was no appetite for constitutional upheaval, on their part or his.

In one department of state, however, it could hardly be avoided. The navy which King Charles inherited had grown to be the most powerful in Europe, but its power rested on fragile foundations. The Interregnum had provided no stable form of naval administration, and no lasting source of finance. The fleet of 109 ships cost £40,000 a month to run, and at Midsummer 1660 the Navy owed £678,000, nearly half of it in unpaid wages to seamen. None of the experiments of the last twenty years offered a satisfactory model for the future of the service.[3]

On 31st May and 2nd June Charles issued Orders in Council temporarily continuing the existing system while a committee of the Privy Council examined the problem. One month later the Lord Admiral's post was revived and the Navy Board reconstituted. The committee had accepted almost unchanged a scheme devised by Sir William Penn, a veteran admiral and naval administrator. The scheme drew heavily on those of Buckingham and Northumberland before the Civil War, and like them it made sure that the Treasurer of the Navy, as the Lord Treasurer's man, could not dominate the board. He was in fact entirely excluded from it, while to weaken its individual members, and strengthen its collective capacity, "all things are disputed publicly, and are either allowed, or reason given to the contrary, and not left to a particular person's appointment, which hath formerly begotten irregularity, confusion, discord and emulation amongst them, and discontent to those that had to do with the service". The general business, according to the new Lord Admiral's instructions, was to be transacted "by Common Council and Argument of most Voices, endeavouring jointly to advance his Majesty's Service". How far His Majesty's service was actually advanced by this arrangement is doubtful, but it served its turn in preventing any one of the Principal Officers from dominating the Board and undermining the position of the Lord Admiral.[4] On the other hand, the new Navy Board was composed, with one exception, of men of experience and ability, and they were clearly expected to fulfil one of their traditional functions in being advisers to the inexperienced Lord Admiral. They were frequently summoned from their office in Seething Lane to attend the Duke in Whitehall. A more distinct connection was established in 1662 when William Coventry, the Lord Admiral's Secretary, was appointed an extra Commissioner at the Navy Board.[5]

In principle the establishment of 1660, with a Lord Admiral advised, if necessary perhaps restrained, by the experienced men of the Navy Board who administered the Navy, was a workable one. In practice things did not follow the plan. The Navy Board in the form of a general council, transacting all business in common, proved quite unable to cope with the rapidly expanding concerns of the Navy. In 1668 the Clerk of Acts* presented the Duke with a paper showing that since 1653 the correspondence of his office had increased sixfold. He charged the Board as a whole with neglecting their instructions to check all accounts and supervise all business. They for their part more or less admitted the charge, and laid the blame on the weakness of the Board's constitution, the pressure of war, and the continual shortage of money.[6]

The weakness and chronic poverty of government were indeed the usual background to all naval administration in the seventeenth century. Though the merchants in the House of Commons constantly

*The former office of Clerk of the Ships, still a Principal Officer, but in effect the secretary of the Navy Board.

pressed for a large fleet, they showed very little understanding of the enormous expense it required. Charles II was always short of money, and the most expensive of all public services was the most severely affected. Determined as he was not to "go on his travels" again, the King did not resort as his father had so unwisely done to the royal prerogative to raise money for the fleet, and so it depended on the willingness of Parliament to grant supplies, and of the King to accept the political conditions so often attached to them. In the long run the greater financial strength of England was to prove the most effective support of her naval power, but this strength was latent rather than apparent in the Parliaments of Charles's reign, suspicious of the royal intentions and ignorant of naval affairs.[7]

It is all the more remarkable that at least twice during the reign the Navy's debt was more or less discharged. "This day," wrote the Clerk of Acts in his diary on 3rd December 1663, "Sir G. Carteret* did tell us at the table that the navy (excepting what is due to the yards upon the Quarter now going on, and what few bills he hath not heard of) is quite out of debt—which is extraordinary good news; and upon the Change, to hear how our Creditt goes as good as any merchant's upon the Change is a joyful thing to consider; which God continue." He did not. Less than two years later naval suppliers were going bankrupt and seamen were starving in the streets of London. This was no mere figure of speech; desperate men besieged the Navy Office demanding their pay, while harassed clerks struggled in vain to conjure it up: "Did business, though not much, at the office, because of the horrible Crowd and lamentable moan of the poor seamen that lie starving in the streets for lack of money—which doth trouble and perplex me to the heart. And more at noon, when we were to go through them; for then a whole hundred of them followed us—some cursing, some swearing, and some praying to us". There were hard winters in those years, too; ships were frozen in their berths at Deptford, and many of the poor and hungry died of the cold.[8]

Shortage of money was the ever-present background to the work of the duke of York, for "this also must be owned, that no degree either of knowledge, good will, or industry in an Admiral can suffice for this work, until an express fund be appropriated . . . . to the Service of the Navy". Yet the Duke did not lack knowledge, industry or good will. He

*Treasurer of the Navy.

was "concerned to mend things in the Navy himself, and not leave it to other people." He worked tirelessly to improve the discipline of the fleet, though constantly hampered by "lack of [money] in the right, and its presence in the wrong places". He laboured to reform the ticket system, by which the seamen were paid in paper notes, encashable at some remote and unspecified date, and susceptible of all sorts of frauds at their expense. Often they would count themselves fortunate to get fifteen shillings in the pound from some broker like Mrs Salesbury in Carpenter's Yard, off Aldgate. Exactly the same sort of discount applied to Navy bills; the longer the "Course of the Navy" (the delay in payment), the more the merchants inflated their prices to compensate themselves, and the more expensive the Navy's poverty became. "The want of money was the root of all evil in the Stuart navy", and against it even "the most mathematick Admirals England ever had" struggled in vain.[9]

The "mathematick Admirals" were James and Charles II, and we must revert to the King to explain why the Duke, though an able and hard-working administrator, knowledgeable and enthusiastic, was yet much less the master of his office than idler and less worthy men had been before him. The fact was that Charles had more than half a mind to be Admiral himself. He too knew and cared a great deal about his Navy, and was not disposed to leave all the fun to his brother. In consequence, the affairs of the Navy, often in great detail, tended to come before the King in Council. The proper dimensions of a new yacht, the propriety of giving a pension to a seamen's widow; nothing was too trivial for the royal attention. Inevitably, with a king skilful enough to lay off the draught of a new vessel or correct Trinity Houses's charts, the Lord Admiral tended to be eclipsed, especially after the disasters of 1666 when Albemarle and Prince Rupert eased him out of commanding the fleet at sea. Moreover the Duke had enemies, notably the earl of Clarendon, Charles's chief minister, who resented the power, or rather perhaps the influence, of the Admiral, and was a sworn enemy of Coventry, the Duke's secretary. Sir William Coventry was a man of great industry and ability, and as a Commissioner of the Navy and of the Treasury, member of the Tangier Committee and of the Committee of Trade and Plantations, and a leader in the House of Commons, he occupied a pivotal position of much value to the Duke.

When Coventry was dismissed all his offices in 1669, it weakened his master's position, already undermined by the defeats of the Second Dutch War. The King, too, was in political difficulties. The Whig opposition was growing more powerful, Parliament less tractable, the King poorer. The status of his brother, an incorrigible Papist publicly installed in an office of great trust and power, was one of the King's gravest weaknesses. In 1673 Parliament passed the Test Act, obliging all holders of public office to subscribe to a declaration condemning Catholicism.[10]

The duke of York was of course the first target of the Act, and Charles had to face the task of replacing him as Lord Admiral without conceding royal control over the Navy. In this emergency he turned to the Clerk of Acts. Of all the members of the new Navy Board of 1660, Samuel Pepys was the only one who owed his appointment solely to patronage and had no previous experience of naval administration. It was an inauspicious beginning for a man whom some consider to be the prototype of the modern civil servant, and the young man was not at first above exploiting his position like any other placeman. Nevertheless, his industry, his extraordinary organizing ability, and his dedication to the service he had undertaken were already so apparent that he had become the trusted adviser of the Lord Admiral. The scheme he devised provided for the office to be put into commission, having first been emasculated. By an Order in Council of 13th June 1673, two days before the Duke resigned, Charles reserved to himself the profits of the Admiralty Court and the issuing of orders to the Navy and the Navy Board. Having thus reduced the office to an insignificant sinecure, Charles placed it in commission.[11]

On 9th July 1673 the new Lords Commissioners for executing the Office of Lord Admiral received their patent. They were in fact the members of the existing Committee of the Navy, set up by the Council in 1668 as a sop to the opposition, and Prince Rupert and his colleagues, if not in all respects the King's men, could hardly be classed with the Whig Opposition. The new Admiralty Board functioned very much like a Privy Council committee, meeting at first in the Council Chamber, later at Hampton Court—not always at Derby House, where their Secretary, Samuel Pepys, had his office. The King generally presided, indeed he had much the best record of attendance; 195 of the 308 meetings of this board. With him often came the duke of York; not, of course, a member of the Board, but still a Privy Councillor and Lord Admiral of Scotland.[12]

By this ingenious scheme a new naval administration was created which in most respects worked much like the old, and left the power of the King and the influence of the Duke little changed. Indeed, by 1677 when the Board was reformed, Charles was taking a greater part than ever before:

> "the despatch of general business thereof being wholly performed by the immediate direction of his Majesty (with the advice of His Royal Highness) to Mr Pepys, the meetings of the commissioners being uncertain, and only in cases admitting delay and requiring the formality of public debate; at which meetings his Royal Highness did, by the King's command, always assist until by his removal out of the land in [1679] (through the malignity of the then times) his Majesty was (to the utmost ruin of his navy) bereft of his brother's further aid therein."[13]

As a board, this new Admiralty must be accounted a disastrous failure, but as a cloak for the personal direction of the King and the Duke, through the agency of Pepys and his clerks, the Admiralty served very well, and the Navy enjoyed the best administration it had ever had. With the wholehearted backing of the Duke, Pepys set to work to bring system and discipline into the Service. Examinations were introduced for midshipmen and pilots, masters and lieutenants. Captains were forbidden to carry freight or go absent from their ships without leave. Pepys was an implacable foe to those like the captain of the *Lark* whom in July 1675 he saw:

> "at a distance sauntering up and down Covent Garden, as I have too often heretofore observed him spending his time when the King's service required his attendance on shipboard, as it doth at this day—a practice which shall never pass my knowledge in any commander (be he who he will) without my taking notice of it to his Majesty and my Lords of the Admiralty."

The temper of the age made it remarkably difficult to enforce such regulations. Good order and naval discipline were constraints scarcely recognized, still less observed, by gentleman captains, "thinking themselves above the necessity of obeying orders, and confirming themselves to the rules and discipline of the Navy, in reliance upon the protection secured to them therein through the quality of their friends at Court". Even commanders-in-chief at sea found it hard to exact obedience; the duke of Buckingham, an officer in Albemarle's flagship during one of the battles of 1666, quarrelled so furiously with his handling of the fleet that he threatened to throw Albemarle overboard. Pepys also had occasion to complain of the King's unseasonable leniency to offenders; "this his Majesty's indulgence. . . is most fatal to his service". Nevertheless, Pepys was in a much stronger position than any naval administrator before him. Not only was he tireless and incorruptible, he had the ear of the King. Sometimes the methodical Pepys found Charles's foibles irritating, but some old canvas for the royal birdcages or a barrel of tar for Mr Rose the King's gardener were a small price to pay for constant support and understanding.[14] It was in these years that Pepys laid the foundations of much of the modern Navy. He instituted a system of rates, standardizing the ships and guns of the fleet. For the first time, provision was made for wounded seamen and their widows. A regular convoy system was instituted in the Mediterranean. The first step towards a permanent corps of officers was taken with the introduction of pensions, and various financial reforms to repair the constant shortage of money were undertaken. Poverty continued to sap all Pepys's efforts, but this too was lessened by generally good relations with Parliament. Pepys had entered Parliament in 1673, specifically as one of the King's men to explain and defend the Navy. With justice he believed that the ignorance of M.P.s of naval affairs was a root cause of much of the Navy's problems:

> "having too many instances before me of the prejudices and disadvantages the affairs of the Admiralty and Navy, and the King's service in both, have fallen into, and with difficulty been afterwards delivered from, for want of timely remedy, which a few hands in Parliament thoroughly conversant in these affairs might with ease enough have administered."

He was now the chief spokesman for the Navy in the House of

Commons, and was justly proud of his success in February 1677 in obtaining a grant of £600,000 to build thirty ships.[15]

The achievements of 1673 to 1679 have been presented as though they were largely the work of Pepys, although he was only the confidential servant of a Board of Admiralty which was itself largely powerless. Paradoxically, Pepys was in a uniquely powerful position. He was completely trusted by the King, who gave his orders directly to the Secretary, often not troubling even to inform the Board. The Navy Board received their instructions from him, speaking in the King's name, "more like an Admiral than a secretary", as his enemies remarked. Though he had only a clerk or two at Derby House, he was in a key position to control the whole administrative machine. Prince Rupert and his colleagues might protest, but real power had passed them by.[16]

In the autumn of 1678 Pepys may well have felt that, although "to regulate and reform the Navy seems a work at this day little less than that ascribed to Hercules in his cleansing the Augean stables", he had at least made a fair beginning, and had a fair prospect before him. Within a year his master the Duke was in exile, he himself in the Tower, and much of what they had achieved in ruins. In the violent storm of the Exclusion Bill and the Popish Plot which burst over the King and his brother, they had to cut and run in order not to be overwhelmed. Inessentials were jettisoned wholesale to lighten the ship of state, and among them were the Admiralty Board and its Secretary. A Parliamentary enquiry brought charges against Pepys of treason and corruption. He was for some time in danger of his life. The Admiralty Board was dissolved as a royal cabal, and the triumphant Whigs demanded that the powers of the Lord Admiral be granted entire to a new Board drawn from among themselves, with but a single Privy Councillor. In these inauspicious circumstances there took office the first Board of Admiralty chosen, in the modern fashion, from among the majority party in Parliament, its members taking seniority, not by their rank at the Council table, but by their order in their patent.[17]

Pepys was horrified:

"No king ever did so unaccountable a thing to oblige his people by, as to dissolve a Commission of the Admiralty then in his own hand,

> who best understands the business of the sea of any prince the world ever had, and things never better done, and put it into hands which he knew were wholly ignorant thereof."

The members of the new Board, led by Sir Henry Capel, had virtually no experience of naval administration, and they at once dismissed Pepys, who might have supplied it. They started with a doctrinaire assumption that the royal administration of the Navy had been corrupt and profligate, and their first action was to dismiss many of the staff of the Navy Office, and order a large programme of shipbuilding for which the money and materials were entirely lacking. The results were inevitable. With "the *effects* of *Inexperience* daily discovering themselves", the morale and efficiency of the Navy sank rapidly. Pepys in his enforced retirement wrote bitterly of the "ignorance, debauchery and other defects" of these "country gentlemen wholly ignorant of the business of the Navy", and even the King "observed to me of his own accord the total unsuccessfulness of the present Commissioners of the Admiralty".[18]

One may well echo Pepys's incredulity that Charles should install a Board about whose incompetence he had no illusions, but he had no alternative. By conceding restrictions on a Papist king and placing a vital part of the government in their hands, he hoped to conciliate the moderate men of the Country party and split the opposition. He may also have hoped to use the new Admiralty to discredit the whole idea of government by commission, opening the way for a resumption of royal direction.[19]

By 1681 the worst of the political storm had blown over, and Charles was able to eject Capel and replace him with the more amenable Daniel Finch. Finch was a member of the Privy Council, but of none of its more active committees, and he was generally passed by. What business he could transact directly, without reference to the Board, Charles did. For the rest, he ignored it.[20]

In 1684 the inevitable Tory reaction in the wake of the discovery of the Rye House Plot gave Charles his chance to dissolve the Admiralty, taking naval affairs into his own hands, with his brother as *de facto* Lord Admiral (or assistant Lord Admiral) under him. Once more Pepys became Secretary, with all the power he had possessed before.

Indeed, his authority was now much higher; no longer the servant of a Board, even in name, he held office as "Secretary for the Affairs of the Admiralty"; not as private secretary to the Admiral like his predecessors, but by virtue of letters patent under the Great Seal. In all but name he was a Secretary of State (neither of the two Secretaries of State ever interfered with naval affairs in his time). There seems little doubt that, like his royal master, he aspired to follow French models of government. Charles envied the absolute monarchy of Louis XIV; Pepys wished to become a "Secretary of the Marine", as he put it, like Colbert. In most respects he had virtually succeeded by 1688. He wielded nearly all the powers of a minister. If he could have secured an Admiralty Committee of the House of Commons, as had existed during the Commonwealth, guiding the House and susceptible of guidance by the Secretary, alleviating the chronic poverty of the Navy, he might in time have succeeded in establishing in England a naval administration curiously similar to that of the United States in the twentieth century.[21]

Charles II died on 6th February 1685, and his brother succeeded. For Pepys it meant very little change. James retained the Admiralty in his own hands, so that it became hardly distinguishable from the kingship itself; the power of Pepys as the King's Secretary for the Admiralty was if anything increased. He needed all his power and assurance, because five years of rule by the Lords Commissioners of 1679 had undone much of his earlier work. The whole naval administration lay in decay and demoralization. The ships rotted at their moorings for want of attention to air them in dry weather, and batten them down in wet. "I have with my own Hands," wrote Pepys, "gather'd *Toad-Stools* growing in the most considerable of them as big as my *Fists*." After an inspection with the Navy Board of Chatham Dockyard in April 1686, Pepys and the King returned by yacht:

> "and we back again from below Gillingham up the river in a violent storm of rain all that evening and night, without one port shut upon any one of the ships in our passage but what we by hailing caused to be so, or upon the *St. Andrew* and *Grafton* in dock, neither shipwright nor assistant, nor any other officer minding it . . . nothing being more evident than the evil that this negligence has brought upon the

> navy by ships being kept with their ports either always shut in dry weather or open in the wet, to the occasioning that succession of heat and moisture which has ruined them."[22]

The results of Pepys's initial enquiry into the state of the Navy had been presented to Charles shortly before he died, and were taken up by James. A year's experience suggested that the efforts of the existing Principal Officers were insufficient, and so, on 26th January 1686, Pepys presented a "Memorial and Proposition from the Secretary of the Admiralty touching the Navy", proposing to replace the Navy Board by a temporary commission, to set the naval administration to rights. In effect this was a strengthened Navy Board under the King's supervision, which was to say under Pepys's, who kept "my daily hand and eye over them". The achievements of this commission were considerable. It was the subject of a hostile scrutiny by the Public Accounts Committee appointed in 1690 to investigate the misdeeds of Stuart government, which reported that:

> "the ships built, rebuilt and repaired by these commissioners were fully and well performed, and the buildings and other works by them erected and made during the continuation of the same commission were done with great exactness, sufficiency and frugality of expense in the managery and conduct thereof."

It "set a standard to which future Parliaments constantly referred in their provision for the annual requirements of the Navy."[23]

By the spring of 1688, with the Commission nearing the end of its work, Pepys was once again in control of an administration of remarkable efficiency for its day. It was about to be put to the ultimate and only real test for any fighting service, mobilization for war. In mid-August James became alarmed at the preparations being made by the Dutch, and ordered the whole fleet to be fitted out. Things did not proceed entirely smoothly. Commissioners had to be sent down to the fleet to take charge, leading to the premature dissolution of the Commission, and the restoration of the Navy Board. The Navy had not, even under Pepys, escaped the inevitable limitations of the age:

> "After a mobilization and a campaign lasting four and a half months, and undertaken in favourable conditions, largely of his own

making, the navy was in debt to approximately half its annual expenditure, its stores were unevenly distributed and in some cases uncomfortably low, its victualling recently proved to be a costly and only partly redeemed failure, its men deserting, unpaid and — as it proved in another few weeks — occasionally mutinous, and the loyalty of its officers profoundly disturbed. That despite all this, it was undoubtedly in a better state than it had been five years before, or was to be one year later, is a sufficient commentary on the conditions in which it operated. The fact that such contrasts could so easily be drawn and that the state of a department and a fleet could apparently show such variation in so short a time, is evidence precisely of the compelling and unchanging circumstances which demanded so great a contribution from personal management. It was by the exercise of individual forethought and energy that Pepys and his associates were able to achieve as much as they did; with their disappearance, the obstacles which they partially overcame again appeared to dominate the scene."[24]

Pepys was a brilliant administrator, who overcame the almost insuperable obstacles of the age; but he was more than this. His career enriched the Navy with the elements of stability and permanence without which it could never have developed into a disciplined fighting service. He endowed the Admiralty with a tradition of impartial service, not to master or patron, not to self-interest or ambition, not even to King or Parliament, but to the Navy itself and its well-being. That Pepys left this intangible but invaluable heritage is all the more remarkable because the Admiralty, as a department of state, can scarcely be said to have come into existence during his career. The total staff in 1687 was seven; four clerks, a messenger and a doorkeeper, besides Pepys himself. All were his personal employees, and had no formal connection with the state's service. Yet more than a century after his death, when the departed servant of a discredited régime had long been forgotten, his diary unpublished and his achievement unknown, his memory was preserved in the Admiralty as "a man of extraordinary knowledge in all that related to the business [of the Navy], of great talents, and the most indefatigable industry."[25]

Pepys lived in age of transition, when the old relationships of politics and administration were breaking down, and new ones had not yet emerged. He was one of the first of the King's servants to have to come to terms with the new power of Parliament. In becoming an M.P. and acting as spokesman of his department he was the precursor of constitutional developments of great moment. In his own eyes, however, he was not the minister of a constitutional monarch; he was, or hoped to be, a "Secretary of the Marine", the powerful servant of an absolute king. He would have been surprised and displeased to hear himself described as the forerunner of an age in which the administration of the Navy would be chiefly directed by Parliament. His extraordinary talents had carried him to an eminence which inevitably involved him in politics, and brought him a seat in Parliament, but he was never a Parliamentary politician; he was the King's man, and the Navy's man.[26] He stood, in a curious paradox, for some things which were already old-fashioned in 1688 and for future prospects which never came to fruition, as well as for others which became central to British naval administration. If James II had ruled into an untroubled old age, Pepys might be remembered as the first British Minister of Marine; as the founder, perhaps, of a political dynasty closely identified with the fortunes of an absolutist monarchy. As it is, this administrator who left no administration behind him has been hailed as the first civil servant, and as the saviour of the Navy. When he handed over his papers in March 1689, no grateful government ennobled its retiring servant, no great ministry lamented its departing chief. The forms of government for which he had contested were never revived, and much of his work was undone by neglect and dissension. Yet he left a monument more durable than any of these; an inspiration, an example, and a tradition of single-minded service to the Navy which the Admiralty never forgot.

Only the most acute and well-informed observer of the political scene in 1689 could have foreseen that Pepys's career was to leave any mark on the future history of naval administration. He was identified chiefly with a form of government by the King and his confidential servants which the authors of the Glorious Revolution were not likely to perpetuate. Much of his service had been under two Boards of Admiralty which had proved unhappy expedients for obscuring the real sources of power. When the King, the Lord Admiral and the

Secretary did the work, the Board had not done much harm. When Parliament had the helm, the results had been disastrous. There was nothing here to suggest that putting the Admiralty into commission was likely to be a fruitful or durable constitutional device. There was equally little reason to suppose that a permanent Admiralty Office was required. Even Pepys had wielded his enormous power with the help of a few personal clerks, and left hardly any organization behind him. The Navy Board administered the Navy, as it had done for a century and a half, and whatever form of higher direction of naval affairs the government of King William settled on seemed unlikely to call for the otiose and possibly dangerous Admiralty Office. The Admiralty as a department of state was at best a sickly and ill-favoured starveling, while to seekers of adminstrative efficiency and to proponents of Parliamentary control alike, the precedent of a Board of Admiralty was repellent.

NOTES

1 Tanner, *PNM,* 264.

2 Sainty, *Admiralty Officials,* 158.

3 Tanner, *Pepys and the Royal Navy* [*PRN*], 37. Chandaman, *Public finance,* 196.

4 Perrin, *Notes,* 33. Penn, *Memorials,* I, 242-243, 591. Tedder, *Navy of the Restoration,* 42-51. Murray, III, 316-318. Tanner, *Catalogue of Pepysian MSS* [*CPM*], 1, 6-7, 24.

5 Murray, III, 318. Tanner *CPM,* I, 19. James and Shaw, 10.

6 Tanner, *CPM,* I, 28-31. Tedder, 49-51.

7 Tedder, 40. Ehrman, *War of William III,* 171-172.

8 Tedder, 46, 54. Tanner, *PRN* 44. Latham and Matthews, IV, 405; VI, 255.

9 Tanner, *PNM* 195, 418; *PRN* 19, 27, 53. Tedder, 57. Latham and Matthews, IX, 258.

10 Murray, III, 321. Robinson, MM XXXVI, 12. Penn, 233. Vale, CHJ XII, 107-109. Tanner, *PNM* 51, 128; *CPM* IV, xcv, ci.

11 Tanner, *PRN* 28-30; *CPM* I, 38-39. Perrin, *Notes,* 33, Murray, III, 322-325.

12 Tanner, *CPM* I, 42; IV, xi-xiv. Ehrman, 193.

13 Tanner, *CPM* I, 38-39; II, ix-xiii. Perrin, *Notes,* 33.

14 Murray, III, 316, 324. Tanner, *PRN* 67, 70, 73; *CPM* IV, lxx-lxxiii, xli-cx. Ehrman, 22.

15 Tanner, *PRN* 27, 31, 48-56, 76; *CPM* I, 49-53, 233; IV, xxv, xli, liii. Ranft, JMH XXIV, 368-374.

16 Perrin, *Notes* 35-37. Ranft, 372.

17 Tanner, *PNM* xix, 181, 197-198; *CPM* I, 57-60; *PRN* 32-33. Murray, III, 326-328. Ehrman, 194.

18 Tanner, *PNM* 71, 116, 133, 357; *PRN* 33; *CPM* I, 61-62. Collinge, *Navy Board Officials,* 3. Aiken, "Conflict & Commission", 208. Murray, III, 326-328. Pepys, *Memoires,* 6.

19 Aiken, 206. James and Shaw, 12.

20 Murray, III, 328-330.

21 Sainty, 34. Tanner, *CPM* I, 58, 65. James, MM XXIII 477; BIHR XVII 20. James and Shaw 168. Ranft 370, 374.

22 Powley, *Navy in Revolution,* 163. Pepys, 47. Tanner, *CPM* I, 87.

23 Tanner, *CPM* I, 66-67, 91-96; *PRN* 34-35. Pepys, 17-33. Powley, 162. Collinge, 3. Ehrman, 206-208.

24 Ehrman, 211-221, 243-244.

25 Ehrman, 196. Sainty, 2. Tanner, *PRN* 16.

26 Ranft, 368. Ehrman, 192, 196.

CHAPTER THREE

BOARDS OF ADMIRALTY 1689-1702

First Lords:

8th March 1689	Admiral Arthur Herbert
20th January 1690	Thomas Herbert, Earl of Pembroke
10th March 1692	Charles, Lord Cornwallis
15th April 1693	Anthony Carey, Viscount Falkland
2nd May 1694	Admiral Edward Russell, later Earl of Orford
31st May 1699	John Egerton, Earl of Bridgewater
4th April 1701	Thomas Herbert, Earl of Pembroke

Senior Naval Lords:*

8th March 1689	Admiral Arthur Herbert
20th January 1690	Sir John Chicheley
5th June 1690	Admiral Edward Russell
23rd January 1691	Captain Henry Priestman
2nd May 1694	Admiral Edward Russell, later Earl of Orford
31st May 1699	Admiral Sir George Rooke

LORDS ADMIRAL 1702-1709

26th January 1702	Thomas Herbert, Earl of Pembroke
20th May 1702	Prince George of Denmark
29th November 1708	Thomas Herbert, Earl of Pembroke

Senior Members of the Lords Admiral Council:†

22nd May 1702	Admiral Sir George Rooke
11th June 1705	Admiral Sir David Mitchell
19th April 1708	David Wemyss, Earl of Wemyss

SECRETARIES OF THE ADMIRALTY 1689-1709

March 1689	Phineas Bowles
January 1690	James Southerne
August 1694	William Bridgeman
26th September 1694	Josiah Burchett (jointly with Bridgeman until 24th June 1698)
20th May 1702	George Clarke** (jointly with Burchett until 25th October 1705)

*The position was not formalized; the senior naval member was often the First Lord, and was not necessarily the principal naval adviser if not.

† Naval members in each case.

**Clarke was Prince George's personal secretary, made joint Secretary of the Admiralty to accompany him on his absences from London.

CHAPTER THREE

Insipid Ignorants

"I wish [the Admiralty Board] eternally confounded, that wee poore country farmers mought injoy our innocent diversions in peace and quiet, and the nation its trade, and more prosperitie then possibly it can under the management of such insipid ignorants, as that Commission is composed of."

Arthur Herbert, earl of Torrington[1]

THE fleet which James II had built and cherished, about which he knew and cared more, perhaps, than any other part of his kingdom, and governed more wisely, failed him in his hour of need. Imprisoned in the Thames by the Protestant wind which wafted William down Channel, baffled by contradictory orders from Whitehall, hampered also by increasing, and increasingly well-founded fears that his officers might prove less loyal to their King than to their faith, Dartmouth, the Commander-in-chief, was unable, or unwilling, to intervene at the decisive moment. A King that understood the sea and cared for the Navy fled in the night, and a foreign monarch, a general and a landsman, rode at the head of his troops down the same streets where the cheering crowds had greeted James and his brother twenty-eight years before.

William of Orange brought to his new kingdom a consuming hatred of the French, and a very slight acquaintance with the English. He came from a nation which had been continuously at war against mighty neighbours for almost all its short history, whose internal politics were characterized by violent faction, sometimes culminating in treason and assassination. He looked on England chiefly as a great accession of strength in the struggle with France, and he was not familiar, nor always very patient, with the constitutional niceties of his new realm. Reserved and even suspicious by nature, he naturally confided in his fellow-countrymen, and few even of them. He valued a man he could trust above a position of importance, preferring "to work through men, and not through their offices". He hated factions and politics, looking to all men of good will to rally to the Protestant cause. There must have been many Englishmen who regretted that the defence of their religion had obliged them to resort to this dour and dictatorial monarch.[2]

The settlement of 1688 was a revolution only in a strictly limited sense. With hindsight the constitutional historian may speak of a decisive change of direction, of the foundation of Parliamentary sovereignty; to the men of the day it was in many respects an unsatisfactory compromise. Revolutions are not made by moderate men with private reservations, nor are they preserved by the judicious conciliation of opposing factions. The uneasy coalition which had installed William was united only in opposing James, and had little positive belief to hold it together. Yet all these men had to be rewarded with offices, though many of them could hardly be trusted with power. So the characteristics of William's government were the multiplication of offices and the concentration of power; the apparent ramifications of the constitution concealing a simple personal government through a handful of trusted advisers.

Parliament, which under the Stuarts had often been an ignorant and prejudiced inquisitor, regarding all aspects of government with suspicion as extensions of the royal prerogative, was drawn in William's reign into a more active participation in administration. As one of the architects of the settlement, Parliament was involved in defending it, and its members had to be given places in proportion to their influence.[3]

The Navy and its governance presented William with particular difficulties. He badly needed the fleet—it was the principal military prize of his new kingdom—but it was also the darling of the Stuarts. He could not afford to shake its loyalty by sweeping purges, yet he must have it commanded by men he could trust. A Lord Admiral was decidedly not wanted; so powerful a position, and one so closely involved in the war, must be reserved to the King alone.

These were the political necessities which shaped the naval administration of the Glorious Revolution. The Admiralty was placed in commission, with a Board chosen largely from the House of Commons and from men whose goodwill was valuable. Naval or administrative experience was not heavily represented. Only the senior commissioner, on whom the King had to depend for leadership and advice in a Service he needed but did not understand, had to be of different metal.[4]

There were only two senior officers in 1689 whose political and professional qualities fitted them to be William's confidential adviser on naval matters. Both Arthur Herbert, created earl of Torrington in May 1689, and Edward Russell were experienced seamen of the appropriate Whig connections; more important, they had both risked their lives in planning William's coming, and had everything to lose if the Stuarts should be restored, so their loyalty was as dependable as it could be in men who had already betrayed one sovereign. They were in that sense political allies, but they were hardly personal friends. Indeed, few men liked Torrington, and his private life shocked even that licentious age: "Of all the worst men living," wrote Pepys, "Herbert is the only man that I do not know to have any one virtue to compound for all his vices." But his political and professional virtues outweighed any want of personal ones, and he became William's First Lord and commander-in-chief at sea.[5]

Seldom can the Admiralty patent, with its theoretically equal distribution of collective responsibility, have concealed such vast disparity between real and apparent power. William's personal government was conducted very largely through the Secretaries of State, whose influence commenced to rise steeply from 1689. They were the usual channels of the King's orders to responsible officials, including commanders at sea, and they did not confine themselves to general instructions or great events. Orders for ships to be fitted, convoys assembled or pensions paid, the minutiae of naval administration, came from them as often as from the Admiralty. The Board at which King Charles had presided and the duke of York advised was never favoured with the presence of the new King. Even in the absence of the First Lord at sea, the Lords Commissioners were not often summoned to advise the King, unless to appease the Parliament. Often the Board was quite ignorant of the whereabouts of the fleet, enquiring pathetically of the Secretary of State for some morsel of news. In August 1693 Pepys heard from his old colleague Sir James Houblon of a meeting with their friend Sir John Lowther, a member of the Board:

> "He told me that Sir John Lowther of the Admiralty came lately to discourse him. When Sir J. H. observing to him between jest and earnest that we were at length come to one improvement in our conduct, namely, of being able to keep a secret, forasmuch as nobody could tell to this day whither our Fleet's last orders were to carry them. . . . Whereto Sir J. L. replied that none could know less of it than they of the Admiralty, the orders not only for their sailing, but even for their victualling going straight from the Cabinet. And this he delivered by way of complaint of their being no better treated than they are in their office, but made when they are called to wait without, as the most ordinary attendants do. Which I cannot reflect on but with the last degree of indignation, when I consider . . . the political absurdity of having so great a trust committed to people whose ignorance or unfaithfulness are by this usage asserted by the State itself that employs them."[6]

It was natural for Pepys to be indignant, remembering as he did at least one Board of competent men, well led and well advised, in actual charge of the Navy. The Board of 1689, however, was not the body to be trusted with this great responsibility. These were not the "Men of estate, quality, credit and reputation; of experience and diligence, zealous of your service, not leaning to faction or favours—and above all, men of temper", for which the Clerk of Acts pleaded so eloquently. Many of them were not often present at the Board. Politics, Parliament or the Court claimed their attendance, and the quorum of three could with difficulty be mustered. Of the 1689 Board, Sir Michael Wharton and Sir William Sacheverell rarely troubled to attend, and Sir Thomas Lee was generally too ill to. With Torrington at sea, only three Lords Commissioners remained to transact the trivia which the new order left them to decide. As a sort of post-office, they were allowed to repeat the orders transmitted to them by the Secretary of State in order to quiet the tender constitutional consciences of parliamentary opponents, but though the hand was the hand of the Admiralty, the voice was the voice of Daniel Finch, earl of Nottingham and Secretary of State for the Northern Department, who dealt with naval affairs. Living down his inauspicious service on the Board of 1679, Finch had acquired some grasp of naval affairs to match his political ability. Under him, a parallel system of command operated which passed the Admiralty by completely. The Lords Commissioners served a political purpose alone, and as an operational body might with ease have been dispensed with.[7]

The impotence of his colleagues only underlined the power of the First Lord. He alone could provide the King with the expert advice which he badly needed, but which they were incompetent to provide. Even at sea matters of consequence were referred to him, and he corresponded directly with Nottingham or the King. As a member of the Cabinet he had no need to refer to others, and his personal nominee as Secretary of the Admiralty kept him well enough informed of the Admiralty's business without often obliging him to attend the Board in person.[8]

Ironically enough, Torrington was indirectly responsible for increasing, at least in theory, the powers of the Board. In June 1690 he was defeated by a superior French fleet off Beachy Head, having been ordered to engage against his better judgement. His enemies demanded he be dismissed and court-martialled, and overriding the protests of the Lords Commissioners against the unwelcome gift, invested them by Act of Parliament with all the powers formerly enjoyed by the Lord High Admiral, lest the trial be voided on a technicality. Thus the theoretical constitutional powers of the Board, if not its practical authority, were increased to meet an unsavoury political necessity.[9]

The bitter factional strife which had led to Torrington's downfall soon embroiled Russell, his successor as commander of the fleet. Taking warning by his predecessor's fate, he refused to accept an order from Nottingham in the Queen's name (William being absent on the Continent) without prior instructions from her. The omission was repaired, but relations were permanently soured. After the victory of Barfleur in 1692, which was criticized as incomplete, and the intended attack on St Malo to exploit it, which proved impossible, Russell refused to attack without specific orders, and Nottingham and the Council declined to give more than general appreciations. The House of Commons, seizing the chance to use the Admiralty as a stalking-horse, took up Russell's cause and demanded real power for the Admiralty, alleging the want of it to have been the cause of all the disappointments at sea.[10]

King William hated this sort of quarrel, and did not much like military failure, however caused. His remedy was to dismiss both Russell and Nottingham and offer the Opposition one of the Secretaryships. Accordingly Sir John Trenchard was put into office "as the least offensive of the Whig candidates for a post that could not be refused them". He had "neither political stature nor experience of sea warfare". The King's Secretary simply ignored him and continued to correspond on naval affairs with Nottingham. Poor co-operation between the two Secretaries of State was a major cause of the disaster to the Smyrna convoy, attacked by the French off Portugal in 1693. When the duke of Shrewsbury took the Northern Department next year he and Trenchard divided sea affairs between them at the Straits of Dover, and flag officers corresponded accordingly. The conduct of naval operations did not noticeably improve, and "the Board of Admiralty was no more qualified than usual to replace or assist its superior".[11]

The First Lord from 1690 to 1692 was the earl of Pembroke, an experienced diplomat whose contacts with the Dutch were of great value in this coalition war, and kept him more often at the Hague than at the Board. His two successors lacked both political and professional weight, and were not Cabinet members. The Admiralty was universally ill-esteemed, and most men acquainted with public life would have agreed with Torrington in condemning its members as "insipid ignorants", though it needed a man with a grievance to attribute so much mischief to such feeble creatures.[12]

Meanwhile Admiral Russell had used his enforced retirement to good effect. The political fortunes of his Whig friends were rising swiftly, and with them his own influence. He was the victor of the great battle of Barfleur which had delivered the country from invasion, and whatever the wrangles which had led to him hauling down his flag in 1692, his success seemed the greater as his successors achieved less. In the spring of 1694 his return to power was completed by his appointment both as commander-in-chief and as First Lord. He was Treasurer of the Navy, Treasurer of the Chamber, and a member of the Cabinet.

His nominee effectively ran the Board in his absence; his secretary became Secretary of the Admiralty.[13]

Soon afterwards, Russell sailed with the fleet for the Mediterranean where, in an audacious and unprecedented feat of logistics, it was to be maintained, far from its bases, throughout the following winter. He left his brother Commissioners in ignorance of his plans. The channels of power and command flowed past the Admiralty as before. Secretaries of State issued secret and weighty orders direct to Russell—indeed, in some sense he issued them himself. He was a member of the Cabinet, and only in the winter, when he was home, were the issues of grand strategy discussed. The orders Russell received were for the most part those he had himself assisted in framing; he commanded in the Mediterranean less as a flag officer than as a supreme commander deputed by the Cabinet. The Admiralty had no part in this. It functioned with the unobtrusive regularity of an administrative body of no political weight. Russell, indeed, with all his power, gained little from being First Lord. It gave him no additional importance, and even £1,000 a year was a trifle compared with the income from the Treasurership of the Navy. Like Torrington before him, Russell was not really a powerful admiral of great political influence, he was a great Whig politician who was both politically and professionally indispensable. In becoming First Lord, "they did not derive importance from their official position, but rather conferred importance upon it".[14]

The status of the Admiralty in fact rose a little in the last years of the war for other reasons. The Secretaries of State during those years were not of outstanding quality, and the authority of the Board, and of the Lords Justices who deputised for the King during his frequent absences on the Continent, recovered a little. The Admiralty even mustered the spirit to dispute with the Lords Justices their authority to give orders to the fleet without consulting the Board. Nevertheless, when the Peace of Ryswick in 1697 brought an end to the war, the Admiralty Board remained a body of no real service to the Navy, and of only limited political usefulness to the government.[15]

It was otherwise with the Navy Board. William's habits of personal government through a small number of trusted servants increased his reliance on efficient administration, which was anyway bound to be acute in time of war. By 1689 the fleet had outgrown the resources of its administration, and it would have been difficult satisfactorily to have met its wartime needs had there been no fresh developments. This war, however, posed new and yet more alarming problems, culminating in the unprecedented requirement to maintain the entire fleet, without a dockyard, in foreign waters throughout the winter. The Board was responsible for an industrial organisation of unequalled size and complexity, "in some respects the largest industry in the country, the greatest shipbuilder, a substantial importer of raw materials, one of the biggest purchasers of agricultural produce and clothing materials, a large medical institution and one of the major employers of labour". In 1694 the central establishment of the Board employed fifty-one clerks, making the Navy Office one of the largest departments of state. By 1704 it had sixty-three. It was well that the members of the Navy Board were in general men of ability and experience. Sir Richard Haddock, who as Comptroller presided over the Board, was already a Commissioner of nine years' experience when he was appointed by Charles II in 1682, and was still in office when he died in 1715, having been Comptroller under six sovereigns. Charles Sergison, Clerk of the Acts from 1690 to 1719, had already served twenty years in the Navy Office when he was appointed. No more than three Surveyors held office between 1672 and 1715; a single Controller of Treasurer's Accounts from 1691 to 1717. This weight of continuity and experience gave the Navy Board in its own field an authority which the Admiralty could not match. The senior Board could be ignored more or less with impunity, but the junior was indispensable to the fleet. As often as not the Navy Board received its orders directly from a Secretary of State without the Admiralty being allowed into the secret. Haddock was a trusted and respected official, consulted by the King's ministers when they would never have troubled themselves with the Commissioners of the Admiralty. Little wonder that the Comptroller, when sounded on the possibility of joining the Admiralty, declined, saying "I know well I am capable of doing his Majesty far greater service as I am, than if I were at that bord".[16]

The Principal Officers had not enjoyed such prestige and power since the sixteenth century, and with the eclipse of the Admiralty, and the absence at sea of Russell who was in all but name Lord Admiral, they began to hope for a recovery of their ancient rights as chief naval advisers to the Crown. They complained to the King of the combative ignorance of the Admiralty Commissioners, "so impatient of contradiction as hardly to be conversible, and uncapable by that means of being informed, and consequently of ever being made masters of a business so intricate as that of the Navy". "The officers of the Navy," complained Sergison, "had been kept from H.M. so long that they had almost forgot they had a King". If William had been as enthusiastic about the Navy as James, they might have made good their claim and restored their ancient position as expert advisers to an amateur Lord Admiral, but it was not to be.[17]

William III's hatred of party warfare, and his determination to tolerate no extreme party men as ministers, were more and more severely tried as his reign continued. The uneasy calm of 1689 broke up into bitter factional struggle, men of moderate politics or none were fewer and farther to seek, and "warm" men, like Lord Dartmouth whom Nottingham described as "party sense in person without respect to the reasons of things", harder to avoid. The great eighteenth-century political parties, the Whigs and Tories, were settling down as identifiable interests, but in the process there was much confusion, bitterness and instability. For all his professional abilities and political standing, Russell (created earl of Orford in 1697) was one of the warmest of party men, and constantly embroiled in factional quarrels. The conclusion of peace in 1697 gave him the liberty to pursue his politics without interruption, and soon matters reached a pitch which William would not tolerate, with Orford demanding the resignation from the Board of Sir George Rooke, not only a very successful sea commander, but just the sort of mild, impartial figure the King wished to have about him. Orford's resignation in 1699, however, did not end the turmoil. Admiral Churchill and Lord Haversham, among other members of the Board, continued to quarrel with undiminished enthusiasm, and in desperation William resolved to dissolve the Board and dispose of them all by appointing a Lord Admiral, the first since the Test Act had obliged the duke of York to resign nearly thirty years before. On 26th January 1702 the earl of Pembroke, a mild, almost apolitical Tory and a former First Lord, received his patent as Lord High Admiral of England.[18]

Two months later William died, and in April war was again declared. Pembroke, conceiving it his duty, prepared to hoist his flag at sea, though he had no sea experience, and by no means always attended the Admiralty for daily business. Nottingham, once again Secretary of State in the new administration, was horrified. Moreover the new Queen's Tory ministry, with Godolphin, Nottingham and the duke of Marlborough (Captain-General of the allied army) forming its inner council, had other plans for the Admiralty. The Queen had it in mind as a proper employment for her husband, Prince George of Denmark, and the profits of the office were looked for the help to pay for the war.[19]

So Pembroke was removed, and in May 1702 Prince George received his patent. The Prince was an amiable man, too gouty to move much, and credited with very little brains. A Council was appointed to advise and guide him, upon which George Churchill, Marlborough's brother, represented the ministerial interest. Prince George's position much resembled that of a modern civilian First Lord presiding over his Board.[20]

Unfortunately for the Queen, her husband was a weak point in the ministry. The war at sea during the War of the Spanish Succession was prosecuted by the French chiefly by commerce raiding, and the heavy losses of English shipping which ensued had direct and immediate political effects in England, through the powerful mercantile interest in the House of Commons. Prince George was commonly presented as a cypher, controlled entirely by Admiral Churchill. The failings of the Admiralty were attacked by the Whigs in particular, who spoke of "the most scandalous management of all . . . never to be cured but by the Prince's quitting, for whatever Council he has, George Churchill will in effect always be lord High Admiral". This sort of attack struck the Queen in a tender spot: "It must needs be very disagreeable to the Queen & particularly uneasy to the Prince".[21]

The Queen's position became still more disagreeable when Nottingham and the High Tories, growing doubtful about the wisdom of pursuing the war, withdrew from the ministry. From 1705 to the winter of 1708 a "non-political" coalition was kept in power, balanced uneasily between Whig and Tory. With the Commons in balance, as in 1705, such a scheme was more or less workable, but it required more skilful leadership than Godolphin's Cabinet could provide, and it could not afford the "dead weight" of Prince George and Admiral Churchill. Moreover the Whigs were gaining strength all the time. The legality of a Lord Admiral taking other advisers than the Navy Board was challenged, and naval strategy dictated by Act of Parliament. The Cruizers and Convoys Act, 1708, required forty-three ships to be removed from the Lord Admiral's strategic control and employed as the Commons saw fit. Queen Anne's position was too weak to fight even this humiliation.[22]

It is probable that in fact Prince George was not as ineffective as contemporaries claimed, and many later writers have accepted. "A prince of a familiar, easy disposition with a good sound understanding but modest in showing it", the Prince attended the Admiralty frequently, and when his health took him to Bath he kept close touch with naval business. Almost all orders he signed in person, and questions of strategy, and even of technical detail, were frequently referred to his decision. Moreover Admiral Churchill, allegedly the real head of the Council, was not by any means the most regular attender, nor the leader in discussion. He seems never to have issued orders by himself—in contrast to Admiral Mitchell, who figures much more largely in the minutes. Both the Queen (who considered him "one of the ablest men for that service that could be found") and his enemies gave Churchill credit for more power than he actually exercised. We may accept that he was "something more than a rapacious and incompetent bird fancier", but he was a good deal less than the evil genius of the Prince of Denmark.[23]

Justly or not, the Lord Admiral remained a source of acute political weakness to his wife. The Whig Junto were determined to restore Orford, and considered that this was one drama from which the character of the Prince of Denmark could with profit be omitted. The Whigs in Parliament in December 1707 mounted an investigation into Admiralty accounts further to embarrass the ministry. Prince George received a new patent as Lord Admiral of Great Britain following the Act of Union in that year, but it was extremely doubtful how much longer the Queen could sustain him, and indeed the whole Marlborough connection. On 19th October 1708 Sunderland wrote on behalf of the Junto demanding the removal of the Prince and the

Admiral, and proposing the restoration of Pembroke as Lord Admiral—he was no Orford, but at least he was politically colourless and not tainted by association with the ministry. Marlborough advised his brother to resign to save the Prince, and thus the Queen. It was too late. On 28th the Prince died, and his Council was automatically dispersed. With the gravest misgivings, Pembroke accepted office under a ministry by now largely Whig in composition. For a year he struggled on with colleagues he found it impossible to work with, but in November 1709 he resigned.[24] The Whigs were in a position to demand that Orford replace him, but the old admiral was prudent enough to avoid taking office as the candidate of a faction which was unlikely to be able to sustain him in power indefinitely. He declined to serve unless the Admiralty were placed in commission, and there was no choice but to accept his terms. So once more a Board of Admiralty hoisted its corporate flag; a Board most unusual in that its three senior members, Orford, Leake and Byng, were all sea officers. The experiment of amateur Lords Admiral had been tried and found to answer neither political nor naval requirements. Henceforward the safe and unexciting alternative of a commission was to be preferred.

In twenty years since the Prince of Orange had seized the throne of England, the authority and importance of the Admiralty had drastically declined. Under the Stuarts, it had served as the vehicle to carry an obscure official to the inner counsels of the monarch. Under William it served as a convenient depository for that sort of political follower in Parliament who had to be placated with office at the least possible expense in administrative inconvenience. Yet, paradoxically, it was under these Boards of "insipid ignorants" that the Admiralty as a department of state was founded. For all his personal authority, Pepys had had no more than a private office of clerks who were his employees, and lost their jobs when he lost his. His influence and example continued as an intangible heritage, but the only direct connection was the books and papers which he reluctantly handed over to his successor in March 1689. These were of the first importance. The archives of any administration are its corporate memory, even in some part its spirit; to inherit them from Pepys was to inherit his method and example.[25]

Pepys's successor in 1689 was Phineas Bowles, whose qualification for the post was simply that he was Torrington's private secretary. In the absence of the First Lord, Bowles would keep his eye on the Board and report to his master. He came as a political nominee, and so he went in 1690, when Torrington was disgraced. His successor, James Southerne, had been Clerk of Acts to the Navy Board since 1677, and involved in naval administration since the Restoration. He was an old associate of Pepys, steeped in his methods, and he brought with him experience and devotion to the Navy. Having been appointed by the Admiralty Board, not by letters patent, he was beyond doubt their servant and not their master, at least constitutionally. Unlike Bowles, he was not a political nominee. He was, however, already an old man, and in 1694 he resigned through ill-health, and was replaced by William Bridgeman, a former Under-Secretary and Clerk of the Privy Council, and another seasoned administrator. Under him the Admiralty's first establishment was laid down. There were two Chief Clerks, six clerks, a messenger, two servants, a porter, a watchman, and the necessary woman.* All were paid by the state: £800 a year for Mr Bridgeman, down to £20 a year for Mrs Buck.[26] Bridgeman also set in train the process of finding a permanent home for the little department. Pepys's Admiralty Office from 1684 had been in his own home in York Buildings, which he declined to part with, so since 1689 the clerks had worked in a variety of temporary accommodation. In 1689 Bridgeman was able to purchase and demolish Wallingford House in Whitehall, where James I's Lord Admiral the duke of Buckingham had lived, and begin a new Admiralty Office, on its present site. In 1695 the clerks were able to move into their new home.[27]

One might well ask how and why this tiny department (less than a tenth of the size of the Navy Office) had come to establish itself successfully when the Board it served was so powerless. In part it may be explained by the abilities of Southerne and Bridgeman, and by the needs of war. The main reason, however, was precisely that the Board was so powerless. Its servants were not sufficiently important to be political appointments, and yet the work of the Board, trivial though much of it was, had to be done. If the Lords Commissioners were "insipid ignorants", they needed competent subordinates to do the work. The Admiralty Office was not completely dispensable, but it was unimportant enough to be quite unobtrusive. Under methodical

*It should perhaps be explained that the "necessary woman" was a housekeeper.

Secretaries, it began to acquire a regular routine for the transaction of of business. The Board met daily in wartime, on Mondays, Wednesdays and Fridays at ten or eleven o'clock for regular business, on Thursdays between six and eight in the evening for applications for employment. Delegations of M.P.s and merchants came to discuss convoys and the protection of trade. Occasionally the Board were summoned to advise the Privy Council; once a week the Navy Board attended for consultations, and on Tuesdays and Thursdays the Admiralty Board waited on the Cabinet if required. A regular procedure was developed for laying papers before the Board and keeping minutes.[28]

The work of the Admiralty Office was largely a matter of the co-ordination of naval policy and administration. The policy was made elsewhere and often passed the Admiralty by; the administration was transacted elsewhere and the Admiralty was hardly competent to oversee it. Nevertheless it played a humble but useful rôle as a centre of communications, filling the gap between grand strategy and administration. Orders, originating from Secretaries of State, were copied and sent on their way to the fleet. Convoys were organized, a work which became more onerous and important after the renewal of war in 1702 brought a *guerre de course*. The Secretary of the Admiralty had to see notices advertising convoys put up in the Royal Exchange, and for the colliers (whose masters did not frequent such august halls) in Billingsgate. Measures had to be concerted by correspondence with bodies in the outports, such as the Bristol Society of Merchant Venturers. The slow communications of the age enforced what would now seem unorthodox measures, as in 1689 when the Provost of Leith was asked to give the Admiralty's orders to take a convoy to the first warship to touch at the Forth, warning the local merchants accordingly.[29]

By such humble but useful service the Admiralty secured for itself a minor but assured place in the administrative life of the Navy. It was worthwhile for Russell, when he became First Lord in 1694, and almost at once sailed for the Mediterranean, to be sure to have his own man in the Office. At first he simply took care that Bridgeman knew that "among the common business of the office you might now and then mix affairs worth his knowing", but that autumn his personal secretary Josiah Burchett was sent home to join Bridgeman as joint

Secretary. Like Bowles before him, Burchett was an entirely political appointment, and he had the unfortunate distinction of having been dismissed by Pepys for taking bribes, but he was to become one of the great Secretaries of the Admiralty, preserver and transmitter of the traditions of the Office for nearly half a century. He was in many ways a political Secretary, whose job was in part to keep his absent master informed of political affairs, and who sat in the House of Commons most of his career. Yet he was also the first Secretary to be recognized as a permanent official, unaffected by changes of ministry. The established structure of the little Admiralty Office was now headed by an established Secretary. Under Pembroke and Prince George, Burchett's influence as the man who controlled and understood the little administration rose steadily. Though he was still an obscure official, and neither powerful nor influential, the Secretary of the Admiralty was already attracting hostile attention from the pamphleteers.[30]

The survival of the Admiralty during the reigns of William III and Anne, when often it seemed that the usefulness of the Board had been ground so fine between the upper millstone of the Cabinet taking decisions, and the nether of the Navy Board and the fleet at sea executing them, that there was nothing left for the Admiralty to do, owed a good deal to the small but efficient bureaucracy of the Admiralty Office. Though the Office was relatively insignificant, and the Board was relatively useless, no substitute for either had proved satisfactory, and there were never enough sinecures to satisfy the claimants on a ministry. So for want of an alternative rather than for any positive merit, the Board of Admiralty survived its beginnings as a political expedient to become a part of the constitution.

NOTES

1 Ehrman, 366.

2 Ehrman, 267-270. Murray, V, 204. Holmes, *Politics in the Age of Queen Anne*, 7, 43.

3 Ehrman, 192, 267-270.

4 James and Shaw, 12. Ehrman, 270-273, 287-288.

5 Ehrman, 270-278.

6 James, BIHR XVII, 20-21. Thomson, *Secretaries of State*, 78-79. Ehrman, 298-305, 403-405. Tanner, *PNM*, 319-320.

7 Merriman, *Sergison,* 8. Ehrman, 288, 296-308, 495. James, BIHR XVII, 14-15.

8 Ehrman, 299-300, 512-513, 556. James, BIHR XVII, 18-20.

9 Murray, I, 27. James and Shaw, 180. Ehrman, 364-365.

10 James and Shaw, 21-22. Ehrman, 410-411. Thomson, 80.

11 Ehrman, CHJ IX, 271-272. Horwitz, *Revolution Politicks,* 143-144. James, BIHR XVII, 23-25.

12 James, BIHR XVII, 18-19. Ehrman, *Navy*, 366.

13 Ehrman, *Navy,* 272, 513. James, BIHR XVII, 19-20; MM XXIII, 483.

14 Murray, IV, 101. James, BIHR XVII, 19. Ehrman, *Navy*, 512-513. 554-556. Sainty, 19.

15 Ehrman, *Navy,* 606-607. Murray, IV, 102.

16 Ehrman, *Navy*, xvii-xix, 269-270, 495. Reddaway, BIHR XXX, 177. Merriman, *Sergison,* 2, 12, 340-341; *Queen Anne's Navy*, 10-11. Murray, IV, 102-103. Collinge, 22.

17 Merriman, *Sergison,* 8-9, 18.

18 Holmes, 19, 43, 405-406. Murray, V, 204. Merriman, *Queen Anne*, 2.

19 James, MM XXIII, 488. Murray, V, 204-205. Perrin, MM XII, 143. Merriman, *Queen Anne*, 3-4.

20 James and Shaw, 12-13. Merriman, *Queen Anne*, 3-4. ADM 2/28 ff. 302, 335-338. ADM 2/29 fo. 230. ADM 2/30 ff. 69-70. (I owe these references to the kindness of Dr John B. Hattendorf).

21 Green, *Queen Anne,* 119, 165, 175-176, 197.

22 Murray, V, 206. Holmes, 71-74, 368-370. James, BIHR XVII, 15. Baugh, *British Naval Administration* [*BNA*] 19. Crowhurst, *Defence of Trade*, 55.

23 James, BIHR XVII, 15. Green, 175-176. Tunstall, *Byng* I, lxvi, lxix. Prince George signed the great majority of orders and warrants in person. For attendance at the Board see ADM3/17-23; for an example of the Prince concerning himself with professional details, see British Library Add. MS 29, 591 fo. 111 (*ex inf.* JBH).

24 Holmes, 111, 141, 370. Green, 165, 197. Merriman, *Queen Anne*, 3. Murray V, 206-207. Tunstall, *Byng* II, xv.

25 Ehrman, *Navy,* 249, 283-285.

26 James and Shaw, 168-170. James BIHR XVII, 17; MM XXIII, 480-487; BIHR XIV, 170-171. Ehrman, *Navy,* 558-565.

27 James, BIHR XIV, 181-182. Ehrman, *Navy,* 566. Smith, MM IX, 274-275.

28 Merriman, *Queen Anne,* 10. Ehrman, *Navy,* 295-296, 495, 554. James, BIHR XVII, 16.

29 James, BIHR XVII, 20-25, Crowhurst, 49, 58.

30 James, MM XXIII, 483-484, 488-491. See p. 53 below.

CHAPTER FOUR

BOARDS OF ADMIRALTY 1709-1770

First Lords:

8th November 1709	Edward Russell, Earl of Orford*
4th October 1710	Sir John Leake*†
30th September 1712	Thomas Wentworth, Earl of Strafford
14th October 1714	Edward Russell, Earl of Orford*
16th April 1717	James Berkeley, Earl of Berkeley*
2nd August 1727	George Byng, Viscount Torrington*
21st June 1733	Sir Charles Wager*
19th March 1742	Daniel Finch, Earl of Winchilsea
27th December 1744	John Russell, Duke of Bedford
26th February 1748	John Montagu, Earl of Sandwich
22nd June 1751	George, Lord Anson*
17th November 1756	Richard Temple, Earl Temple
6th April 1757	Daniel Finch, Earl of Winchilsea
2nd July 1757	George, Lord Anson*
17th June 1762	George Dunk, Earl of Halifax
18th October 1762	Hon. George Grenville
20th April 1763	John Montagu, Earl of Sandwich
16th September 1763	John Perceval, Earl of Egmont
15th September 1766	Sir Charles Saunders*
11th December 1766	Sir Edward Hawke*

Senior Naval Lords:*

8th November 1709	Sir John Leake
4th October 1710	Sir George Byng
30th September 1712	Sir John Leake
14th October 1714	Sir George Byng
16th April 1717	Matthew Aylmer
19th March 1718	Sir George Byng
30th September 1721	Sir John Jennings
1st June 1727	Sir John Norris
13th May 1730	Sir Charles Wager
21st June 1733	Lord Archibald Hamilton
13th March 1738	Lord Harry Powlett
19th March 1742	Lord Archibald Hamilton
25th February 1746	Lord Vere Beauclerk

*The position of Senior Naval Lord (under various titles) became generally recognized during this period, and First Lords, though often naval officers, held office for largely political reasons. I have therefore marked the naval First Lords (thus *) in the first list, and given their *next* senior naval colleagues in the second. It should be borne in mind that in many cases the senior naval lord, on either definition, was not in fact the principal naval adviser.

†In his own view, Leake was Senior Naval Lord "acting in the absence" of the First Lord.

18th November 1749	George, Lord Anson
22nd June 1751	Sir William Rowley
17th November 1756	Hon. Edward Boscawen
6th April 1757	Sir William Rowley
2nd July 1757	Hon. Edward Boscawen
19th March 1761	Hon. John Forbes
20th April 1763	Richard Howe, Viscount Howe
31st July 1765	Sir Charles Saunders
15th September 1766	Hon. Augustus Keppel
11th December 1766	Sir Piercy Brett
28th February 1770	Francis Holburne

Secretaries:

26th September 1694	Josiah Burchett
29th April 1741	Thomas Corbett (jointly with Burchett until 14th October 1742)
30th April 1751	John Cleveland
18th June 1763	Philip Stephens

Samuel Pepys, by Kneller, about 1689 *National Maritime Museum*

Thomas Corbett *P.S.A. Photograph Library from the portrait in Admiralty House*

Josiah Burchett peeping out of his periwig

P.S.A. Photograph Library
from the portrait in Admiralty House

John Cleveland.

P.S.A. Photograph Library
from the portrait in Admiralty House

The present Admiralty building seen from Whitehall soon after its completion; engraved by Thomas Bowles
Guildhall Library

The rear of the Admiralty viewed from across the Park in 1759

Museum of London

Sir Philip Stephens in old age, attributed to Beechey

P.S.A. Photograph Library from the portrait in Admiralty House

Lord Sandwich, engraved after Zoffany *National Maritime Museum*

Sir Evan Nepean *P.S.A. Photograph Library, from the portrait in Admiralty Hous*

CHAPTER FOUR

Stationary Officers

> "Whosoever conns the ship of the Admiralty, the Secretary is always at the helm: he knows all the reaches, buoys and shelves of the river of Parliament and knows how to steer clear of them all. He is the spring that moves the clockwork of the whole board, the oracle that is to be consulted on all occasions; he sits at the Board behind a great periwig, peeping out of it like a rat out of a butter firkin."
>
> *Anonymous Pamphleteer*[1]

THE Board of Admiralty returned to the constitutional stage in 1709 for want of a better alternative, and so for some years it remained; not useful enough to have friends, not troublesome enough to have enemies. The election of 1710 brought a Tory triumph and the retirement of Orford and his colleagues, but a new candidate for the Admiralty was hard to find. The claims of Admiral Sir John Leake, the senior member of the new Board, were unanswerable, but he so far disliked the political rôle demanded of the senior commissioner that he absolutely declined it, preferring to be "Second Commissioner acting in the absence of a First", and taking every opportunity to hoist his flag at sea.[2]

The new administration was enthusiastic about the employment of sea power, but Leake's abdication left them without a professional adviser. Undaunted by their ignorance, St John and Dartmouth, the Secretaries of State, planned to improve on the capture of Port Royal by a daring stroke against Quebec. This expedition was conceived without any professional assistance; Leake and the Admiralty were deliberately deceived about its object, and even the Navy Board was only partially informed. In the interests of security the squadron was allowed to sail insufficiently victualled and without many items essential to its success. In the event, only the French were fully informed where it was going. Not surprisingly, the result was a disaster.[3]

When the earl of Strafford joined Leake's Board as First Lord in 1712 St John was understandably anxious to make it clear that "the employment of First Commissioner of the Admiralty brings your lordship into the Cabinet". A headless Board had proved an unfortunate precedent, but it was probably well that the preliminaries of peace at Utrecht had been opened, for Strafford was hardly the man to give the much-needed leadership. The death of Queen Anne in 1714 deprived him of the chance, because all Tories were at once dismissed from the Board, and even, in the case of Sir James Wishart, from sea command. Only the Secretary was left, to serve once again his old patron Lord Orford, now for the third time First Lord. Thus the accession of George I to the throne, followed by that of Robert Walpole to power, brought an Admiralty even more ruthlessly subordinated to political expediency than before. In this it did no more than reflect the tensions of the age. Party government was now firmly established, with the Whigs as the natural governing party of the Hanoverian succession, and the Tories hated and feared by them as little more than Jacobites. Neither sea command nor a seat at the Admiralty were given to any but supporters of the ministry, so Boards of Admiralty "came and went for reasons only remotely connected, if at all, with the conduct of naval operations or administration". Under Walpole, civilians formed the majority of the Board, and a single naval member, frequently the First Lord, provided the Cabinet with expert advice. Even when other sea officers sat at the Board, they ranked as politicians, and no more.

> "The First Lord or Commissioner of the Admiralty is in effect Lord High Admiral, having the supreme Direction of the Board, and disposes Affairs at his Pleasure, except that no Orders of Commissions are valid sign'd by him alone, it being necessary for two or more to sign with him; notwithstanding which he is not to be controul'd by them."

The younger sons of Whig landowners were scarcely in a position to do so. Walpole turned an already political Admiralty into a largely civilian one, involving it intimately in the politics which in that century coloured all administration.[4]

It was an age of violent faction, yet played out within very narrow limits. Walpole's enemies could rejoice in "our honest Admiral's triumph over Sir Robert and Spain"—in that order. Even bishops of different politics seldom associated, and divisions among churchmen were deep and bitter. Yet these were internecine quarrels within the Whig ascendancy; the essential fabric of the Hanoverian succession was not in question. Behind and beneath the turbulence of politics, there was a stability amounting almost to social torpor. Apart from the brief alarum of 1745, there was no time after the defeat of the 1715 rebellion when the Whigs seemed seriously challenged, though they were never so completely secure that they could relax.[5]

The Jacobite threat, distant but never altogether negligible, was one reason why all administrations were agreed on the importance of a strong fleet. The Navy had thwarted the Stuarts in 1690, and might at any time have to do so again. Moreover the mercantilist understanding of economics, and the mercantile interest in the House of Commons, agreed in supporting limited but profitable wars for the conquest of lucrative colonies.[6]

Even more important than the support of the ruling politicians was the revolution in the national finances which gave that support effective expression. The foundation of the Bank of the England in 1694, and the issue of the first perpetual annuities in 1715, allowed government debt to be funded with an ease which alarmed many contemporaries and amazed them all. The absolute regularity of the Course of the Navy made the Navy Bills excellent debt instruments, "In effect, the navy created its own transferable notes". From time to time Parliamentary grants funded the Navy's short into the nation's long-term debt. In the immensely expensive business of running a fleet the financial strength of Britain, and the solid political will to exploit it, were the Navy's greatest assets.[7]

Though the politics of Georgian England were based on fundamental agreement, among other things on the need of a navy, there was little ease or stability in the daily world of public affairs. Civilians were in general hostile to the military world, and unprepared to purchase efficiency in the armed forces at the expense of any risk to their liberties.[8] Above all, this world of turbulent politicians, united in fundamentals and divided by interest rather than principle, could be kept in order only by the great apparatus of patronage which formed the sinews of the Georgian body politic. Only by involving every post in the administration's gift, however humble, in the effort to attract a working majority could the King's government be carried on. Patronage was a reflection of the weakness of central government, which is not to say that it was synonymous with inefficiency. Rather it was the means by which administrators and statesmen balanced their desires and opportunities. The Admiralty relied on it as much as the government, for interest was the only strong hold they had on the loyalty of many of their officers. Men who had powerful friends and relatives—to whom, no doubt, they owed their advance—could be tempted by rewards, but hardly terrified by punishments. They themselves were patrons; every admiral and captain had appointments to dispose of, and consequently influence to employ. Inevitably the Navy was involved in the world of patronage, and therefore politics.[9]

Nevertheless, it remained a world of its own, only in part susceptible to the influence of even the most powerful statesmen. The British constitution by the latter part of the century "resembled a coral reef. It was made up of the skeletons of innumerable offices and functionaries which had served their turn; but inside this dead structure new creatures burrowed, made their home, and turned the detritus of ages into some kind of working instrument." The Navy did not on the whole conform to this pattern. It was an organization of a complexity, efficiency and size unmatched in its age; it could not afford many incompetents. A man who used his influence to promote unworthy officers found their failures redounded to his discredit; the patron of men of ability, on the contrary, prospered by their success. So the Navy was in a measure insulated from the full force of political patronage, generating within itself a system of professional patronage, politically influenced, of which the Board of Admiralty was the centre.[10]

The fact that all patronage ultimately stemmed from the Admiralty was its chief strength, and the chief reason why its effective influence steadily increased. The functional value of the Admiralty remained relatively slight. As before, it neither controlled the administration of the Navy nor formulated policy. The Cabinet handled the central direction of the nation's affairs, including the overall supervision of naval operations. It could and did treat the Admiralty as entirely subordinate if it did not ignore it altogether. Anson's voyage round the world was planned without reference to the Board, and the admiral, for his part, reported primarily to the Secretary of State. Admiral Vernon did the same when in command overseas. Even the First Lord or senior naval lord was not necessarily the Cabinet's sole professional adviser; Sir John Norris was summoned to the Cabinet in 1739 as an additional expert.[11] Anson was in effect senior naval lord as the most junior naval officer on the Board. A weak First Lord could be circumvented or bullied by his subordinates, as when Admiral Mathews, commanding in chief in the Mediterranean at the beginning of the Seven Years War, used his parliamentary influence to force the Secretary of State to put pressure on Lord Winchilsea. Pitt sometimes sent secret orders, especially to the commanders of combined operations, without consulting any other authority, and, as a celebrated anecdote tells us, when he did require the Admiralty's signature, "he wrote the instructions himself, and sent them to their Lordships to be signed, always ordering his secretary to put a sheet of white paper over the writing. Thus they were kept in perfect ignorance of what they signed." We shall see that there is reason to doubt this story, but it did not exceed the possible limits of an eighteenth-century Board's subservience to its political masters.[12]

The long years of Sir Robert Walpole's ascendancy as Prime Minister were years of peace, in which only a single fleet action was fought, but Walpole not only kept up a large fleet, but used it as his principal diplomatic weapon, not hesitating to mobilize it to overawe foreign powers. Disclaiming any knowledge of sea affairs, he relied on Sir Charles Wager, a seasoned administrator with experience as Controller before he became First Lord. Wager was an able man of equable temper, prepared to recommend Admiral Vernon for an overseas command at the same time as Vernon was caustically attacking him in Parliament; "he is certainly much properer than any officer we have to send, being well acquainted in all that part of the West Indies and is a very good sea officer, whatever he may be, or has been, in the House of Commons."[13]

When Walpole was ousted by Carteret's group of malcontent Whigs in 1742, and Wager with him, old Sir John Norris declined to serve either at the Board or at sea. A feeble ministry appointed a feeble Admiralty, led by the earl of Winchilsea, a son of the earl of Nottingham, whose abilities were not so considerable as he thought, and who lacked any naval adviser of merit. His policies were unpopular, not least among sea officers, some of whom, like Mathews, could in effect ignore if not overrule the Board. Mathews's quarrels with his colleague Lestock were largely responsible for the failure off Toulon in 1744, and a weak Admiralty, "associated with a weak and fumbling ministry", was unable to assert effective control. In desperation old Sir John Norris was for a few bizarre weeks made Commander-in-Chief in home waters with the powers of a Lord Admiral. The Admiralty protested, Norris resigned, and as the war intensified Carteret's "Drunken Administration" collapsed. [14]

The Broad Bottom ministry which succeeded in 1744 was as unlike Walpole's in its naval policy as could be. He had relied on Boards of nonentities headed by a naval officer of great experience, and often age, such as Wager or his predecessor Lord Torrington. The new Admiralty had a couple of senior officers, but they were included as the brothers of Whig dukes. Real power rested in three men: the First Lord, the duke of Bedford; his close friend and political colleague the earl of Sandwich; and Captain George Anson, their old ally, now a public hero after returning from his desperate voyage round the world. Bedford, Sandwich and Anson were aged thirty-five, twenty-seven and forty-eight respectively, and Anson was the oldest man on the Board. Here was a Board of young and self-confident men, resting securely on a strong ministry. Though Bedford transacted much of his business by post from Woburn, he was not a figurehead. When he became Secretary of State in 1748, Sandwich succeeded him, and in 1751 Anson himself followed. From 1744 to 1762, with one year's exception, these three ran the Admiralty. They were all determined and able men, Anson especially, and under them the Admiralty Board began for the first time in its history to challenge the right of the Navy Board to administer the Navy with only the most formal supervision. At Anson's instigation the Admiralty investigated ship design, stirred up the dockyards—and in the process stirred up the Navy Board. The

Comptroller, Haddock (son of the old Sir Richard who had been William's Comptroller), and the Surveyor, Acworth, were both in their seventies, and did not take kindly to interference by eager young men of half their age, and half their experience. Sir Jacob Acworth had entered the naval service under Charles II, and if his bodily strength had ebbed, his will-power was unimpaired.[15]

Though the details of the quarrel need not concern us, and a compromise was in effect reached, it was of great significance, because it marked the beginning of a sustained Admiralty attempt to bring under control a body whose subordination had hitherto been little more than a constitutional fiction; and, by no coincidence, the beginning of nearly a century of steadily deteriorating relations between the two.[16]

It was a truism of eighteenth-century government that only a weak administration allowed the Admiralty to take control of naval policy. Anson did so, not as First Lord but as one of the leading members of the ministry. As confidant of the duke of Newcastle, and son-in-law of Hardwicke the Lord Chancellor, he was a man not to be trifled with. He could "withstand recommendations of interest or favour", in his father-in-law's opinion, "more than any First Lord of the Admiralty was ever known to do". He could curtly refuse the patronage requests of the duke of Newcastle, and demand and receive an apology from him for attempting to glean naval information behind his back. His enormous moral, political and personal authority make a nonsense of the suggestion that Pitt, for all his undoubted habits of centralizing the direction of war in his own hands, could force Anson and his colleagues to sign orders sight unseen. Pitt's political position depended upon success, and for success he depended on leaders of Anson's calibre, at the Admiralty and at sea. Anson, indeed, both as a junior commissioner and as First Lord, hoisted his flag at sea and led fleets to victory. In 1761, the year before he died, he had the unique distinction as First Lord, and, in effect, First Sea Lord, of hoisting the Union flag at the main topmast head as an Admiral of the Fleet and commander-in-chief at sea.[17]

It cannot be too strongly emphasized that Anson's unparalleled authority owed almost everything to his political position, and not to being First Lord. Nevertheless, he had achieved his political eminence at least in part because his professional abilities were invaluable, and in time indispensable, to his allies. It is hardly possible, and would to contemporaries have been hardly conceivable, to separate political and professional aspects of his power. He himself thought nothing of enclosing political circulars from the Prime Minister in his Admiralty correspondence with flag officers who sat (as most of them did) in the ministerial interest in the Commons. Yet Anson, with his remarkable prestige, alternated with a First Lord, Lord Temple, (installed by Pitt in 1756 when his brief triumph drove the entire Newcastle connection from office) who was a nonentity, and left the Board entirely under the control of Admiral Boscawen, the senior naval member. Anson himself, when Sandwich became First Lord for the first time in 1748, aged thirty-one, was assured by his new superior that "I would not lose a moment to desire that you would consider yourself as in effect the head of the Admiralty . . . it is my meaning to throw my share of the power, and the direction of the whole, as much as possible, into your hands." Plainly the standing of a First Lord depended more on the man than the office. Anson was succeeded after he died by four civilian First Lords in quick succession (including Sandwich for the second time), and then for four years by Sir Edward Hawke, whose reputation as a sea commander stood as high as Anson's, but whose political standing and administrative ability did not. It can be claimed for him that he managed to obtain more money for the fleet than Anson had found politically possible (or thought politically desirable) but in the opinion of those best qualified to judge he left a paper fleet for his successors.[18]

The standing of the First Lord varied widely, according to the character and weight of the man. Under Temple and Sandwich the First Naval Lord ran the Board; Winchilsea saw his father's system of control by the Secretary of State revived to his own discomfort; but Anson was able to treat a chief minister with a brusqueness verging on contempt, leaving him complaining petulantly that the Admiralty "does not love to be controlled or even advised". No office of profit under the Crown, whether it was Anson's as First Lord or Mrs Clack's as necessary woman, was wholly free of political influence and consequence. Often the professional and political significance of a post, especially one like the Admiralty which was both technical and vital, could not in practice be completely separated. Though Anson was succeeded by lesser men, he endowed the First Lordship with a potential authority which it never lost. His success, where others had failed, showed that the noble amateurs who made up the ministries of Georgian England could not be trusted with entire responsibilty for this, the most complicated, and potentially the most dangerous of the government's responsibilities, at least in wartime. Moreover he demonstrated the strength of the Admiralty as a political base. All patronage in the Navy, which employed as many people as the rest of the government service combined, lay ultimately with the Admiralty, and Anson controlled it absolutely. In spite of, or even because of the fact that he promoted able men regardless of their politics and connections, the master of so much patronage was a man whom no eighteenth-century government could treat lightly. Nor was this the end of his importance. The Admiralty disposed of ten boroughs, and had influence in many more. Most flag officers sat in Parliament, and generally in the government interest. In 1761, of thirty admirals, twenty were M.P.s and one a Scots peer. Many junior officers also sat in the House. By upbringing, and by their position as experts in a profession which the political world could neither comprehend nor do without, they were of independent temperament, even if they were not well-connected, as so many senior officers were. The Navy was something of an *enfant terrible* of Georgian politics, and the man who could control it was both necessary and potentially dangerous to a ministry; possessed of a power too uncomformable to be entirely comfortable. After Anson that power, though it might not be exercised, could never be entirely forgotten.[19]

The power of the First Lord had hardly anything to do with the actual work of the Admiralty Office, but inevitably, as his standing rose, so did that of the Board's little secretariat. Throughout the century it remained very small. Besides the Secretary and his immediate deputy the establishment provided for eight clerks, plus a varying number of unestablished extra clerks which occasionally rose as high as ten. In 1760 there were three messengers, a porter, three watchmen, a necessary woman and the gardener. In the Marine Department were three more clerks, and in the Marine Pay Office another. With legal officials the total employees of the Admiralty in London numbered less than forty. The Navy Board in that period employed up to nine thousand, and the Victualling Board had seventy-four London officials in 1747. The work the Admiralty clerks did was laborious but routine. Much of it consisted of copying orders and letters, issuing passes and protections, making out commissions and warrants, organizing convoys, dealing with the endless appeals for employment or promotion. A table of business drawn up in 1759 details the work of each clerk. Virtually all were engaged chiefly in writing, which in the days before any mechanical means of copying was the main occupation of all clerks. They came to work at eleven and stayed until four, taking it in turns to arrive early at nine (four a day) or to return after dinner and work from six until ten, or later if the work required it. The evening toil was usually the copying of orders to go out by the last post. Four clerks came in on Sunday from nine until four, and again in the evening. One of the senior clerks had an allowance of twenty guineas a year for living near the Admiralty to attend to urgent business during the night. Some received allowances for translation work or other special duties. Pensions and sick-pay, though not formally established, were almost invariably granted on a generous scale. The salaries ranged from £400 a year for the Chief Clerk to £50 for the most junior unestablished clerk, to which should be added fees which might double a clerk's actual income. Promotion among clerks was strictly by seniority, excepting only to the Secretaryship, for which both merit and influence were required. The system may be seen in operation in a minute of 1773:

> "Memorial from Mr James Alcock, one of the clerks in this office, who has been in it thirty years, requesting leave to resign. In consideration of his long and faithful service and of the infirmities he labours under, he is to be allowed a pension of £75 a year, being equal to half his salary. The junior established clerks to rise in seniority and Mr Charles Wright to be appointed to the vacancy of youngest established clerk. . . . Mr Parker to be appointed to abstract and examine the journals of the captains and lieutenants and make out the certificates for them in the manner Mr Alcock used to do. Mr Wright to succeed to every other part of the business lately executed by Mr Alcock. Mr Needham Smith to be appointed an extra clerk in this office".[20]

This picture of a little ministry about its daily routine may seem quite unremarkable, but it was in fact most unusual in its day. The Admiralty demanded and received from its clerks a dedication highly untypical of the Georgian civil servant. In return they were paid extremely highly, with rewards and benefits which would amaze any modern government employee. To work all one's life for a single office, rising steadily by faithful service through successive grades each more highly paid and more responsible than the last, to rely on seniority without influence, to work long hours for high pay, were very unusual for an eighteenth-century government employee. It would not be too strong to say that the Admiralty was already running a miniature civil service of the modern type a century and more before sobriety and diligence replaced influence as the first requirement for an office of profit under the Crown.[21]

The Admiralty clerks began the century in the building in Whitehall which had been put up in King William's time. It was, like all Whitehall buildings in the days before the Embankment was built, very damp and occasionally lapped by floodwaters. Worse, it was by the 1720s in a state of increasing decay, and it became evident that further repairs were likely to prove a vain expense. Consequently the old building was in 1723 demolished and another built in its place. There it stands to this day, wretchedly ill-proportioned and disfiguring a noble site, with its unremarkable rear view across Horse Guards, where the Admiralty garden once lay, and its dingy courtyard on the other side "deservedly veiled", as Horace Walpole put it, by the remains of the Adam screen. This screen, the only external feature of the building which could ever have been called beautiful, was erected in 1760 at the orders of Admiral Boscawen to protect the courtyard from riotous seamen. Boscawen and his celebrated wife Fanny had an artistic judgement not typical of all naval officers, or their wives, and they had just given the young Scots craftsman his first major commission in England at Hatchlands, where their new house was building, so it was no doubt to them that the Admiralty owed one of its few architectural merits.[22]

Admiral Boscawen, like other Lords Commissioners, was expected to work a good deal harder than the placemen on most Georgian boards. Even in peacetime, as a junior lord under Anson (though admittedly one of great ability, and much trusted) he worked two or three days a week at the Board. As *de facto* First Lord in 1756 he was barely able to get away to his family in the country on Christmas morning, and was back at his work on the 27th. Among the Lords Commissioners, political nominees though they were, the circumstances and demands of Admiralty work tended to make them, like the clerks, more professional and involved in that work than their contemporaries elsewhere.[23]

The link between the politicians of the Board and the clerks of the Admiralty Office was the Secretary. He read all the incoming correspondence, and answered it, in their Lordships' name or his own. Only about one letter in five was actually referred to the Board, and the Secretary judged what should and should not be laid before it. He controlled the administration of the Office, and he acted as political manager for the First Lord, looking after the Admiralty's extensive patronage, and managing naval affairs for the ministry in the House of Commons, in which he invariably sat. It was a position of crucial importance, and it was almost unique in eighteenth-century politics. Under-Secretaries in general enjoyed a status in the body politic not unlike that of the chaplain to a noble household; "they had to know a great deal, and not expect too much, to be qualified to sit at the table of their chief, and, in most cases, to be satisfied with the lowest places at it." They were the private servants of the Secretaries of State, until 1770 paid by them, and attending them personally. They left office, of course, when their masters did, which was frequently. The American Department had seven Under-Secretaries in fourteen years of existence. Even the Secretaries of the Treasury, who controlled a large and important administration, changed almost as often. On the other hand "The Secretaries in this Office", as the Parliamentary commissioners observed with approval of the Admiralty in 1787, "contrary to the custom observed in the other Departments into which we have enquired, appear to be Stationary Officers". Nothing is more striking than the very long terms of office of eighteenth-century Admiralty Secretaries. Josiah Burchett, appointed in 1694, retired in 1742. His successor, Thomas Corbett, died only nine years later, and the next Secretary, John Cleveland, in 1763, but Philip Stephens then held office until 1795, before becoming a Lord Commissioner for another eleven years. Four successive Secretaries spanned more than a century, one of them holding office for thirty-three years, and another for forty-eight. In that century, from 1694 to 1794, there were sixteen Secretaries of the Treasury and seventy-six Under-Secretaries of State.[24]

The Secretaries of the Admiralty were in a sense political appointments, and all owed their advance to powerful patrons. Burchett had been Russell's clerk, Corbett Sir George Byng's, Cleveland and Stephens were protégés of Anson. Nevertheless, all were administrators of long experience in naval business before they were appointed. Burchett had begun as a clerk under Pepys. Corbett had been eleven years at sea and twenty-seven in the Admiralty Office when he became Secretary; Cleveland, whom Anson brought from the Navy Office, had worked there since 1722. Even Stephens, the least experienced Secretary on appointment, had worked twelve years in the Navy Office and then twelve years in the Admiralty. When he entered the Navy Office in 1739 one of his superiors, the Surveyor, had served Charles II, and the Secretary of the Admiralty had been trained by Pepys. This was not merely a notional connection with the previous century, but one understood and felt in the Admiralty and the Navy Board. When the Comptroller in 1781 wished to make a point to the First Lord with peculiar emphasis, he could find no stronger support than to quote at length from a letter written by Pepys one hundred and five years before. It is not too much to say that two generations of civil servants linked the Navy of Rupert and Monck with the Navy of Nelson; the Restoration with the Regency. In any age and circumstance this would be a singular record; in Georgian England it marks out the Admiralty as a unique institution.[25]

This combination of the professional authority of long experience in the affairs of the Navy with considerable political consequence gave the Secretaries of the Admiralty a weight out of all proportion to the apparent importance of their office. When we read Corbett thanking his old patron "as you have raised me from the awkward boy you found me, to much better preferments than I could ever have in prospect", we seem to hear the authentic voice of the eighteenth-century placeman; when we hear Lord Halifax declining to accept the First Lordship in 1762 until he was sure Cleveland would be remaining as

Secretary, we have a different image. In 1759 Cleveland declined an invitation to dine from the duke of Newcastle, on the grounds that Boscawen the senior naval lord was dining with him that night. We can hardly imagine the greatest of twentieth-century Secretaries, Sir Oswyn Murray, declining an invitation to dine with Baldwin because earl Beatty was dining with him, though Murray was the cardinal figure in an administration thousands strong, and Cleveland had an office of less than fifty. No twentieth-century Secretary, for all his administrative value, disposed of the political importance of his Georgian predecessors. There was "a vulgar opinion that Cleveland is Lord High Admiral", which could never have happened to his successors two centuries later. Nor was the vulgar opinion wholly misplaced. As early as 1727 the members of the Board casually went off to the country leaving the Secretary with sundry orders "to be sent away, in case the Service should require it". There was no doubt that he had the authority to do so, as Captain Hamilton of the *Augusta* learnt in 1744 when he rashly complained of a letter from Corbett "too much in the stile of an Order from the Lords". "Every Expression of the Secretary's Publick Letters," he was sternly told, "always contains or Implies their lordships' Orders, and is Capable of no other meaning, and has been always so understood by the Officers of the Navy." It was alleged in Wager's time that "the first commissioner being much advanced in years Depends wholly upon ye advice of his Secretary who Prime Minister like, transacts business frequently without Applying to his Master." The status of the Secretary may be roughly gauged by his income from salary and fees, which in 1785 stood as £2,146, more than double that of any Lord Commissioner save the First Lord, and three-quarters of his.[26]

It is all the more remarkable that these wealthy and politically powerful men were accepted as non-political. No doubt Burchett survived the 1714 purge more as an old servant of Orford's than of the Crown's, but by the time he retired after nearly half a century in office, having served and guided two Lords Admiral and twenty-eight Boards, the tradition was firmly established. In 1779 the earl of Bristol, delivering a bitter attack on the then First Lord, excepted from his strictures Mr Stephens, "The most diligent, most intelligent, and indefatigable man in business I ever knew, and from whose absence or sickness I am not at all surprised at anything that may happen to go wrong". Stephens was at that moment engaged in preparing his master's defence.[27]

A highly political office, in a highly political age, was yet excepted as a strictly professional post. The paradox is typical of the Admiralty in the eighteenth century. Its political and administrative functions and fortunes were inextricably intertwined; its strength in one strengthened the other. Its standing in the body politic could not possibly be justified on its administrative usefulness—huge areas of naval affairs (notably finance) still lay completely outside its control—and yet it is true to say both that without its importance to ministers its control over the Navy could not have increased as it did; and that it owed that importance in part to its handling of naval affairs. The curious situation of the Secretaries epitomises the Admiralty as a whole; political figures of great importance, who were nonetheless "stationary officers".

NOTES

1 James, MM XXIII, 488.
2 Murray, V, 207-208. Merriman, *Queen Anne*, 3-4.
3 Graham, *Walker Expedition*, 12-20.
4 Murray, V, 208-212. Baugh, *BNA* 64, 73.
5 Ayling, *Elder Pitt*, 66. Holmes, 21, 28-29, 405.
6 Baugh, *BNA*, 15-19; *Naval Administration* 1715-50 [*NA*] xiv. Ayling, 224.
7 Baugh, *BNA*, 451-473, 496; *NA*, 454-457. Dickson, *Financial Revolution*, 399-400.
8 Baugh, *BNA*, 8, 504.
9 Baugh, *BNA*, 6, 123-125. Finer, PA XXX, 340-341.
10 Finer, 334. Ayling, 244. Baugh, NA, 5; *BNA*, 123-125. Namier, *Structure of Politics*, 33.
11 Baugh, *BNA*, 64-65; *NA*, 1-5. Thomson, 83-88. Williams, *Anson's Voyage*, 3, 8. Pack, *Anson*, 123. Ranft, *Vernon*, 39, 95, 306, 309. Temperley, EHR XXXI, 293.
12 Baugh, *BNA*, 69-70. Pack, 208. Middleton, *History* LV, 189.
13 Murray, V, 211-212. Baugh, *NA*, xii-xiii, 6-7, 15; *BNA*, 66-67, 495-496, 503.
14 Murray, V, 214-216. Baugh, *NA*, 7; *BNA*, 68-70, 503-504.
15 Baugh, *BNA*, 71-72, 503-504; *NA*, 47. Murray, V, 217-223.

16 Murray, V, 209, 222-223. Baugh, *BNA*, 83-91; *NA*, 4.

17 Baugh, *NA*, 2; *BNA*, 71, 88-89. Murray, V, 215-217, 221. Namier, 33. Pack,185, 247. Middleton, *History* LV, 190-193.

18 Namier, 32, Aspinall-Oglander, *Admiral's Wife,* 225. Pack, 176. Murray, VI, 329-332. Mackay, *Hawke,* 301-332. Mackesy, *War of America*, 167.

19 Murray, V, 213, 217. Ayling, 182. Middleton, *History* LV, 194. Namier, 31, 141. Baugh, *BNA*, 6.

20 Wickwire, AHR LXXI, 20. James, BIHR XVI, 25-27. Sainty, 102. Baugh, *BNA*, 55, 63, 75. Crowhurst, MM LVII, 167. Wickwire, HLQ XXVIII, 239. Baugh, *NA*, 11. ADM 3/51, 9th Sept. 1745. ADM 3/54, 9th June 1746.

21 Wickwire, AHR LXXI, 21-24, 30-31.

22 Smith, MM IX, 274-275. Lord Winster, *Political Quarterly* XIII, 233. Aspinall-Oglander, 248.

23 Aspinall-Oglander, 147, 226.

24 Wickwire, HLQ XXVIII, 241, 243, 249. Namier, 37. Wickwire, AHR LXXI, 20, 30-31. Sainty, *Office-Holders* I, II & V (Treasury, Secretaries of State and Home Office Officials), Robert Beatson. A *Political Index to the Histories of Great Britain and Ireland* (London, 1806), I, 408.

25 Tunstall, *Byng* III, 43-44. James, BIHR XVI, 24. Wickwire, HLQ XXVIII, 247. Collinge, 92, 141. Barnes and Owen, *Sandwich* MSS IV, 380.

26 Tunstall, *Byng* III, 43-44. Namier, 41-42. Aspinall-Oglander, 209. ADM 3/36, 29th August 1727. ADM 3/47 fo. 236. Baugh, *BNA*, 67, Wickwire, HLQXXVIII 239, 244.

27 Baugh, *BNA*, 83. Wickwire, AHR LXXI, 24.

CHAPTER FIVE

BOARDS OF ADMIRALTY 1770-1815

First Lords:*

12th January 1771	John Montagu, Earl of Sandwich
1st April 1782	Augustus, Viscount Keppel*
30th January 1783	Richard, Viscount Howe*
16th July 1788	John Pitt, Earl of Chatham
19th December 1794	George, Earl Spencer
19th February 1801	John Jervis, Earl of St Vincent*
15th May 1804	Henry Dundas, Viscount Melville
2nd May 1805	Charles Middleton, Lord Barham*
10th February 1806	Charles Grey, Viscount Howick
29th September 1806	Thomas Grenville
6th April 1807	Henry Phipps, Lord Mulgrave
4th May 1810	Charles Yorke
25th March 1812	Robert Dundas, Viscount Melville

First Naval Lords: †

2nd February 1771	Augustus Hervey, later Earl of Bristol
12th April 1775	Sir Hugh Palliser
23rd April 1779	Robert Man
22nd September 1780	George Darby
1st April 1782	Sir Robert Harland
30th January 1783	Hugh Pigot
31st December 1783	John Leveson Gower
12th August 1789	Samuel, Lord Hood
7th March 1795	Sir Charles Middleton
20th November 1795	James Gambier
19th February 1801	Sir Thomas Troubridge
15th May 1804	James Gambier
10th February 1806	John Markham
6th April 1807	James, Lord Gambier
9th May 1808	Sir Richard Bickerton
25th March 1812	William Domett
23rd October 1813	Sir Joseph Yorke

Secretaries and First Secretaries:

18th June 1763	Philip Stephens
3rd March 1795	Sir Evan Nepean
21st January 1804	William Marsden
24th June 1807	William Wellesley Pole
12th October 1809	John Wilson Croker

*Sea officers marked thus.

† Treating all First Lords as civilian.

Second Secretaries:

13th January 1783	John Ibbetson
3rd March 1795	William Marsden
21st January 1804	Benjamin Tucker
22nd May 1804	John Barrow
10th February 1806	Benjamin Tucker
9th April 1807	John Barrow

CHAPTER FIVE

Shaking the Tree

"If the public officers, on whose orders every preparation and movement depends, are not diligent, regular and punctual, it is of little consequence what your admirals and generals are."

Sir Charles Middleton [1]

IN JANUARY 1771, John Montagu, fourth earl of Sandwich, was appointed First Lord. He had already served on nine Boards, four of them as First Commissioner, but he was only fifty-four, and he was to remain eleven years in office. They were eleven of the most momentous years of the century. When Sandwich returned to the Admiralty, Britain possessed a great overseas empire; when he left she had been decisively defeated in a colonial war for the first time in a century, not only by her old enemy France, but by the unknown and perturbing forces of a nation in arms. The empire was no more, and with it had gone many of the old certainties.

The American War was in British politics, and in naval administration, an era of transition. It was the last of the limited wars of the century, fought by civilized powers for restricted ends, by rules understood and respected by all. Like the earlier wars, it was fought largely in faraway countries whose fate touched the statesmen of Britain more in their pockets than their persons. With some exceptions amongst colonists and savages, it was fought by gentlemen, and by gentlemanlike standards. It was a war for the possession of territory, not for overthrow or revolution.[2]

Nevertheless, it was a war unlike those that had gone before. In the first place, it was a defeat for Britain, and defeat, even in a limited war, has social consequences. It was a defeat, moreover, inflicted in part by a revolutionary spirit of social upheaval, of defiance and revolt, of the overthrow of established orders. Nothing so extreme as revolution happened in Britain (nor perhaps in America), but the political world in Westminster was deeply divided by it, and Lord North's ministry faced by an opposition of a new and unsettling kind. He controlled a typical ministerial coalition of the day, cemented chiefly by patronage, but the Rockingham Whigs were that rare thing in the eighteenth century, an opposition with an ideological programme, united in wanting not only to despoil their enemies of their places, but to reverse their policies. Even without such orators as Burke, Sheridan and Fox they would have been a dangerous force; with the stimulus of defeat in America they grew ever more formidable, and more bitter. Party feeling ran higher than it had done since King William's time, and none were more partisan than naval officers, many of them rough, censorious men, lacking the urbanity of London politicians, and ever ready to suspect their opponents of treachery. Never before had party spirit divided officers at sea as it did during the American War. In earlier and later conflicts feelings ran less high, or the peril of the nation ran higher. The combination of bitter political faction based on principle, as well as interest, with defeat in war, yet in a fundamentally stable society, was a potent one. The Rockingham Whigs were out for reform, as well as power, and they had no inhibitions about damaging the war-effort to get them. There were, as Admiral Rodney remembered of this period, "officers of high rank and unquestionable courage, who nevertheless bore so inveterate an animosity to the Administration then existing, particularly to the First Lord of the Admiralty, the earl of Sandwich, as almost to wish for a defeat if it would produce the dismission of ministers".[3] The main target of the opposition was the patronage system which supported the government, and not least the "Tree", as the Admiralty was familiarly known. "Reports are gone about of the immense profusion of the public Treasury; of the enormous emoluments of some places; of large sums not accounted for; of a vast expense in favouring contractors. . . . and providing for a useless set of men".[4]

To attack the patronage of the Crown, though it be done solely with the idea that the power of the Crown had increased, was increasing and ought to be diminished, had wider implications than a change in the balance of political strength. It necessarily involved distinguishing between the efficient and parasitical parts of the constitution; it implied views on the proper number, salary and employment of the servants of the state. The views, moreover, were those of members of Parliament. Throughout the century, they had been trusted by successive ministries with as little information as possible, and had responded by attacking indiscriminately all arms of administration as tools of ministerial power. To attack patronage rather than patrons involved a definition of what constituted political and what civil service; in short, it implied a distinction between service to ministers and service to the Crown which had never before been made in this form. The change, like any change of attitudes, was the work of many years, but its beginnings can securely be dated to the American War.[5]

The most characteristic political device of this period of transition was the commission of enquiry. Throughout the great wars which closed the century, this remained the most effective weapon by which ministries might be attacked and defended. Ostensibly all these commissions subscribed to the new call for probity and efficiency, all denounced corruption and incompetence wherever they found them: in practice all tended to find them among their opponents. These new weapons, though used to fight the old battles, foreshadowed the ruin of the old order. It was impossible to attack extravagance, corruption and waste, however partisan one's motives, without in the end undermining public complacency and precipitating change.

The earl of Sandwich, to whom it fell to guide the Admiralty and the Navy through these troublous times, was one of the most singular men ever to have presided at the Board. "A tall stout man," thought Fanny Burney, "and looks as furrowed and weather-proof as any sailor in the Navy; and like most of the old set of that brave tribe, he has good nature and joviality marked on every feature"; "his awkward, careless gait", another observed, made him seem to be walking down both sides of the street at once. In society and politics, he was a man of great charm and tact, adroit and imperturbable. With his Parliamentary following of seventeen, founded on the patronage he controlled at the Admiralty and East India House, he had built "a species of political citadel", and his abilities and temperament were framed to exploit it.[6]

He was a scholar of some achievements in the study of classical inscriptions, an enthusiast for oriental languages and an adept in European; a passionate supporter of voyages of exploration. He loved unconventional sports such as fishing, yachting and skittles; he was the leading cricketer of his day and an indefatigable organiser of amateur dramaticals. As a young man he had borne arms against the Pretender (in the regiment commanded by the then First Lord, the duke of Bedford) and he had two sons and a brother serving at sea.[7]

Sandwich may be said to typify the best of the noble politicians of the age, born to a political rôle, but complete amateurs in administration. When he first sat at the Admiralty Board in 1744 he had no experience of, nor connection with the Navy save by inheritance from his great-grandfather, Pepys's patron. Nevertheless, by 1771, whether by acquired ability or inherited genius, Sandwich

> "was universally admitted to possess eminent talents, great application to the duties of his office, and thorough acquaintance with public business. . . . In all his official functions he displayed perspicuity as well as despatch. No naval officer who stated his demand with becoming brevity ever waited for an answer, and he was accustomed to say, 'If any man will draw up his case and put his name at foot of the first page, I will give him an immediate reply. Where he compels me to turn over the sheet, he must wait my leisure'."

Lord Sandwich," another contemporary recalled,

> "might serve as a model for a man of business. He rose early and till a late dinner dedicated his whole time to business; he was very methodical; slow, not wearisome; cautious, not suspicious; rather a man of sense than a man of talent; he had much real good nature; his promises could be relied upon."

Even that bitter opponent of North's ministry, Horace Walpole, conceded that "No man in the Administration was so much master of his business, so quick or so shrewd". He understood more about the Navy and its administration than any civilian who had presided at the Board since James II. He knew and cared about such details as the proper way to repair a dockyard store, or the usefulness of worming rigging. Unlike many professional First Lords, he did not disdain the minutiae of stores and reserves. When he arrived at the Admiralty he found the timber stocks exhausted and "a total despondency at the Navy Office as to the means of procuring it". In 1770 there were

11,813 loads of timber in stock; by 1781, at the end of a greater and more demanding war than Britain had ever undertaken, there were 58,117 loads in stock and a further 22,000 due on contracts in force; the equivalent of over three years' consumption. This sort of unromantic toil was the backbone of any success at sea, and in such affairs Sandwich excelled. Labouring long hours at his desk, sustaining himself with pieces of cold meat clapped between slices of bread, Sandwich became the master of the Admiralty and the Navy as no civilian First Lord had ever been before, or was ever to be again. In the Cabinet, he dominated discussion of naval matters more completely than even Anson had done. Lord North, the Prime Minister, was a man of peace; cultured, charming, adept at political manoeuvre, and incapable of leadership. He inherited a government bereft of direction by the death of the elder Pitt, and, as he admitted pathetically, "I found it so and had not the vigour and resolution to put an end to it". Sandwich wanted neither vigour nor resolution, and by the time the French entered the war in 1778 he was in effect war minister, the author and director of British strategy. Having served his Admiralty apprenticeship with Anson, he learnt to exploit the strength which the Admiral had shown to lie hidden in the First Lord's office. The novelty of Sandwich's position was that he as a civilian had acquired the same grasp over both political and professional detail that had made Anson so formidable, for almost all eighteenth-century admirals were politicians, but very few civilian politicians were admirals.[8]

The American War presented Britain with the enormous and unprecedented problem of supporting armies on a distant continent. The scale of supplies necessary to sustain such an effort was out of all proportion to anything of which ministers had experience, and the protection of these long and vulnerable lines of communication, especially after France joined the war, was a continuing strain on the Navy. The system of naval adminstration which had to meet the challenge was hardly changed from that which the political accidents of the Glorious Revolution had established ninety years before. The principal function of the Admiralty was to co-ordinate the policy of the Cabinet and the activities of the numerous bodies involved in running the Navy and naval operations, but it was not really in a position to perform even this limited function efficiently. In the spring of 1778 the Cabinet ordered Byron's squadron with reinforcements to sail for New York as fresh troops for Halifax, which was also threatened, were on their way already. In fact they were still swinging round their buoys in the Clyde, the Admiralty having detained them without telling Lord George Germain, the Colonial Secretary. Possibly this was an example of Sandwich's off-hand treatment of his Cabinet colleagues rather than the weakness of the administrative machine, but it was not unique. In 1782 the Transport Service only learnt of the impending evacuation of the armies from America (which it would have to undertake) when the Comptroller read about it in the newspapers. Even when the system worked properly, it was cumbersome in the extreme. In May 1780, for example, the Ordnance Board desired to despatch to America their chartered transport *Brilliant*, freighted with Ordnance stores and a party of Engineers. Though she was in all other respects an Ordnance responsibility, the victualling of the troops fell to the Victualling Board. Consequently the Secretary of the Ordnance Board wrote to the Under-Secretary of State requesting him to move his master to approach the Admiralty. The Secretary thereof laid the letter before their Lordships, who ordered him to write to the Navy Board, which after similar deliberations instructed the Victualling Board to cause their officers to issue the necessary orders. This was a perfectly routine procedure, but it was naturally slow. In 1778 the combined efforts of the Admiralty, the Navy Board, the Treasury and the Secretary of State took seven months to ship two hundred butts of vinegar from Deptford to New York. Not less than four departments each had its own sea-transport service; the Navy Board, the Ordnance Board, the Victualling Board, and the Treasury, which chartered army victuallers. In 1779 the Treasury relinquished this charge to the Navy Board, leaving only three departments bidding against one another, pushing up prices which were already increased by the shortage of shipping, and leaving the Navy Board, whose credit was the weakest, in the worst position.[9]

The Navy Board was weak in other respects. The men of long experience who had led it at the outbreak of the Seven Years War had been succeeded by a swift succession of lesser men. Captain Maurice Suckling, who was Comptroller at the outbreak of the American War, was weak of health and character, and the great size of the Navy Office did little to compensate for the declining stature of its leaders. The Cabinet, for its part, was ill-fitted to guide the strategy of a nation at war. Its decisions were generally taken after dinner, frequently with half the members asleep. The minister whose responsibilities were under discussion presided, and if he were Sandwich, usually had his way. Yet none was more eager for the new doctrine of collective responsibility, which dissipated the odium of defeat, and cloaked the exercise of leadership.

> "Every expedition," he emphasised, "in regard to its destination, object, force and number of ships, is planned by the Cabinet, and is the result of the collective wisdom of all His Majesty's confidential ministers. The First Lord of the Admiralty is only the executive servant of these measures, and if he is not personally a Cabinet Minister he is not responsible for the wisdom, the policy and the propriety of any naval expedition. But if he is in the Cabinet then he must share in common with the other Ministers that proportional division of censure which is attached to him as an individual. In no situation is he more or less responsible to his country than his colleagues for any misconduct that flows from the Cabinet measure."

The constitutional principle was of great importance, but it can seldom have been less real in practice than at that time. "Your lordship will require and direct . . .", the Cabinet's orders began, but most often the First Lord had himself decided the tenor of the orders he was to receive.[10]

It was possible for the Admiralty, or its head, to be as "wayward and independent" as this because there was no real control, by Cabinet, Treasury or Parliament, over the Navy's financial resources. The Treasury gave a formal approval to the Navy Estimates, but it had neither power nor information enough to keep any effective check on them. The control of Parliament was equally fictitious so long as the Navy could accumulate its own debt by issuing interest-bearing Navy Bills. Only the Navy Board kept any accounts, and they on a very singular system. When a Treasurer of the Navy left office all ships' books had to be transcribed anew, and the process of clearing his account could not begin until the last ship had paid off. The last ship's book of Lord Grenville's account was not made up until 1771, nine years after his resignation, and this was only the preliminary to the Treasurer's quietus. In 1780 the Navy Pay Office, short-staffed and overwhelmed by war, had brought the annual accounts down only to 1758. While a Treasurer's books lay uncleared, his cash balances remained in his hands. In 1780 the heirs of viscount Falkland owed £27,611 on the account of their ancestor, who had left office in 1689. The financial affairs of the Navy were almost completely out of control.[11]

The feeling that the Navy, the Admiralty, and above all the First Lord were ungoverned and ungovernable was a potent engine of resentment against Sandwich. Worse, he did not play the political game by the rules. He used his position to advance his friends, which in itself was entirely acceptable, but he brought up men of no political weight, on no better ground than ability. When Sandwich resumed office in 1771 Sir Hugh Palliser was a Commodore; by 1778 he was a Vice-Admiral and third in command of the Channel Fleet. Lord Mulgrave was rescued from half-pay and installed in the Commons; his brother was made a post-captain at twenty-three. Flag officers were outraged at what they saw as a direct assault on their professional rights. Nor did it help Sandwich that he selected on merit not only young men who of necessity were his followers, but established commanders like Howe and Keppel who were already his sworn enemies. Party spirit ran so high that men of undoubted courage refused to face a foreign foe lest they give comfort to a domestic enemy. The disastrous quarrel between Keppel, a leading member of the Rockingham Whigs, and Palliser, his second-in-command, after the Battle of Ushant in 1778 split the Navy into irreconcilable factions. Sandwich prudently held that "in the present state of our political system, and the weakness which I perceive in government, who, I think can bring no inquiry into the misconduct of their generals or admirals to a fair or impartial decision, it is most for the good of the whole to avoid public enquiries", but he was unable to prevent a celebrated court martial, with all the inevitable consequences of feuds publicly conducted.[12]

The quarrels of admirals held the attention of the nation, but another quarrel was brewing which was to be of far more consequence for the future of the Navy. In August 1778 Captain Charles Middleton became Comptroller, head of the Navy Board and Sandwich's principal coadjutor in prosecuting the war at sea. It was an office of great importance: "The Comptroller . . . is the main-spring belonging to everything that is naval: no price can purchase a man fit for this extensive office: he must be in every part of it, and know everything that is going on, in and out of it." Middleton was such a man. "The Comptroller," one of his clerks wrote, "is the most indefatigable and able of any in my time. The load of business he gets through at the Board, at the Treasury, at the Admiralty and at his own house, is astonishing, and what I am confident no other man will be able to execute." In his abilities and energies he was a match for Sandwich, who genuinely admired him, but in all other respects they were wholly unlike. If Sandwich was in some ways the epitome of the eighteenth century, Middleton was a harbinger of the nineteenth. The son of a minor Scots customs officer, he had risen by his talents alone, and knew it. Narrow-minded, priggish and arrogant, he considered himself to be the ablest administrator of his day, and he did not mistake. He was a devout Evangelical, with a perhaps characteristic tendency to equate moral probity with practical ability. He believed in God and in himself, and thought obstacles to either one were obstacles to the other.[13]

Such a man was bound to be a difficult colleague, and it is a tribute to Sandwich's restraint and tact that they got on as well as they did. Middleton did not hesitate to attack the First Lord as idle and inefficient:

> "The cause of every disorder, my lord, is in the admiralty, and till a reformation is begun there, no good can be expected from any other quarter."
>
> "For want of plan, for want of men of professional knowledge used to business to assist at the admiralty, and for want of method and execution, one error has produced another, and the whole has become such a mass of confusion, that I see no prospect of reducing it to order. All I can do at the navy office will avail but little if the admiralty continues what it is at present."

The Comptroller was not afraid to instruct the First Lord how to dispose of fleets and commands. Middleton despised Sandwich, not only for indolence, but for immorality. The Countess was insane, and Sandwich lived openly with his mistress and family, to whom he was devoted. In Middleton's mind, inefficiency and depravity were natural associates: "where there is no religion, there can be no public principle". In the face of all these onslaughts, Sandwich remained conciliatory but firm.[14]

Like other men of his character and ability, Middleton's favourite remedy for inefficiency was to take over the work himself. The Victualling Board, the Transport Service, the naval part of the Ordnance Office, were all objects of his ambition. He campaigned ceaselessly for a seat at the Admiralty for the Comptroller, and for a seaman as First Lord—meaning himself. "He got his seaman in the Cabinet in the end; it was Keppel. A short experience of Keppel as First Lord persuaded him that the head of the Admiralty should be a politician, with a statesman's power to support his subordinates and a landsman's humility in naval matters." In truth Middleton disliked all masters, and though his ambition was generally in the interests of the Navy, it was also in his own. He criticised Sandwich as indolent, yet he himself was not as tireless as he liked to believe; he accused the First Lord of jobbery, but he himself leaned heavily on his connections with Dundas and Shelburne, used his influence at East India House, and solicited appointments for his relatives.[15]

It is easy to dislike Middleton, who, as a modern Secretary of the Admiralty wrote, "appears to us as a prig and a bore of the first water". Nevertheless, he was unquestionably one of the greatest civil leaders the Navy has ever had, and his career, as Comptroller, as Lord Commissioner, and finally as First Lord was crucial to the history of the Admiralty and the Navy. For most of the eighteenth century the Navy Board had gradually lost influence to the Admiralty. Middleton went over to the offensive with a determined attempt to wrest final control of dockyard appointments from the Admiralty; equally firmly repelled by Sandwich. This was not just an administrative issue. As the associate of Shelburne and Dundas, soon to be Pitt's confidential adviser, Middleton was the Rockingham Whigs' man in the naval administration. His attack on Sandwich, in his eyes and theirs, was not simply efficiency against indolence; it was honesty against jobbery, merit against privilege, religion against immorality, reform against entrenched corruption. This quarrel did not die with Sandwich or Middleton, but set the tone for the relations between the Admiralty and the Navy Board for half a century, and ultimately had momentous effects on both.[16]

In March 1782 Rockingham and his friends finally achieved power, and Sandwich left the Admiralty for the last time. In the same year a Commission on Public Accounts was appointed, with power to call persons and papers. In 1785 another and stronger Commission, on Fees in Public Offices, took up the work. Their principles were eloquent of the new spirit of the times; there were to be no deputies and no sinecures, no fees or perquisites, no public monies or public papers retained for private advantage. These were startling proposals, but perhaps not as revolutionary as they sounded. The Commissioners' aims were to cut costs and reduce the influence of the Crown by abolishing sinecures and inflated salaries, rather than to overturn the whole system. Moreover the Commissioners were not disinterested. Pitt was by now Prime Minister, and Middleton was his confidential adviser on naval affairs. The connection gave him power, and he did not neglect to use it. Lord Howe was First Lord, but the Comptroller made it quite clear to him which of them really enjoyed the Prime Minister's confidence. The Commissioners, willing to have their work done for them and their report given a tone certain to be acceptable to the Cabinet, hastened to assure Middleton that they would follow his guidance.[17] The Commission reported that the Navy Board was overburdened, that it should have a stronger staff, and that the Comptroller should be unequivocally in charge, becoming "a sort of executive officer to the First Lord and really more powerful than the Sea Lords of the Admiralty". For the moment he did not press his ultimate ambition to get a seat at the Admiralty. The Commissioners' report was completed by 1788, but its embarrassing revelations were less palatable to an established government than to an eager opposition, and they were not published. For three years Middleton urged his cause with relentless determination and repeated threats to resign, until to his fury one of them was accepted in 1790.[18]

Middleton continued as unofficial adviser to Pitt, but he was not a man to whom influence without responsibility was attractive. For the moment he seemed to have closed his naval career, but in 1793 Britain found herself at war again as a member of the First Coalition. This was no limited war to gain a few sugar islands, it was a war of survival against the terrible forces of Revolutionary France, against conquest and social destruction. The politicians of Britain, like the nations of Europe, were thrown together. The luxury of faction was discarded by almost all save Fox and his few associates. Pitt was preparing to reconstruct his government by bringing in the Portland Whigs. The Navy had been found ready for the ordeal of war, and much of the credit had, very properly, gone to Middleton. In these circumstances Pitt installed him as a Lord Commissioner in May 1794. For years he had hoped for this, but his position as junior lord, without his old power as Comptroller, was a bitter disappointment to him. Far from dominating the Board, he was obliged to accept the authority of the earl of Chatham, Pitt's brother, the First Lord. Chatham was not devoid of ability, but he was "surely the laziest man ever to hold a British Cabinet office". When he left office hundreds of unopened public letters were found at his home. Middleton began to wish Sandwich back again. However, a desperate war was raging, and an incompetent brother was a luxury Pitt could not afford, so in December 1794 earl Spencer became First Lord.[19] Though he was only thirty-six, Spencer's birth and wealth had already placed him in the inner circle of the Whig aristocracy. He was in some ways another Sandwich—like him a scholar, with the finest private library in Europe at Althorp—and Middleton found himself no nearer real power than before. Every onslaught Spencer imperturbably blocked with the bulwark of collective responsibility:

> "The idea I entertain of the constitution of this board, and of the manner in which the business of it should be carried on, is that in every measure determined upon and officially proposed to the board by the first lord, every member of the board is considered as ready to take an active part by his signature; and though the responsibility unquestionably rests on the first lord, the other members are always understood to concur in his measures."

For Middleton this was extremely galling. In November 1795 his discontent came to a head over the Cabinet's demand that Laforey, commanding in the West Indies, should be relieved. Chatham required

Middleton's signature to the order, and he resigned rather than give it, "because I know myself amenable to a much higher tribunal than any on earth". So Sir Charles Middleton left the naval service; for good, as it seemed, for after this second resignation, earthly tribunals were unlikely to give him another chance.[20]

Meanwhile Pitt's government, even though strengthened by the Portland Whigs, was beginning to be attacked as heavily as its predecessor, and with the same weapons. A Select Committee on Finance, appointed in 1797, was investigating government offices to see if they had followed the recommendations of the Commission of 1785. Their proceedings with the Admiralty are nicely illustrative of the strengths and weaknesses of the new approach when applied to an independent and well-entrenched department. The pension fund proposed by the Commission had not been established, nor had fees been pooled. The clerks had been graded by seniority, but that only gave formal sanction to a long-standing practice. In the face of the Select Committee's proposals, the Admiralty reluctantly agreed to abolish fees, but absolutely refused to pay the salaries proposed. The Commission, it observed magisterially, "either very little understood or did not well consider the nature and extent of business to be conducted by this Department . . . . where business must be executed at all hours and cannot for a moment be delayed". The Admiralty was determined that its clerks should enjoy a secure and highly-paid employment, with the status of gentlemen. Their contentions were adopted. Salaries were granted 50 per cent or even 100 per cent above those proposed by the Commission, with higher pensions. In 1797 the total salary and contingency bill of the Admiralty had been £41,000; by 1806 it was £43,000. Such was the effect of Parliamentary economy without Parliamentary control of finance.[21]

Though the accession of the Portland Whigs in 1794 left Pitt's government with hardly any formal opposition, his Irish policies, being unacceptable to the King, undermined his own position, and in March 1801 he resigned, shortly before the exhaustion of the combatants brought an end to the war. Addington, the new Prime Minister, invited Lord St Vincent to fill Spencer's place. St Vincent was one of the greatest sea commanders of the age, but he was unusual among admirals in having had hardly any political career. He had never sat at the Board and he had little acquaintance with naval administration. He shared the common prejudices of sea officers, in particular in believing that "the Civil Branch of the Navy is rotten to the very core". For them every failure in victualling or supply was the result of the criminal sloth and corruption of naval administrators ashore. There was of course widespread corruption, but sea officers hardly appreciated the unprecedented problems of supplying huge fleets kept at sea winter and summer in every quarter of the globe. St Vincent was an autocrat, and age had not improved his temper. He had no time for consultation with colleagues, and could never understand why Spencer had bothered to have three naval lords: "It is incomprehensible to me why he keeps more than one seaman at the Board, for they do nothing but confound, impede and distract. . . . The fact is that Lord Spencer is now a better officer than any of the three ever was." His political sympathies were markedly whiggish, and he held them with that naive inflexibility which comes from want of political experience. Accommodation was betrayal in his eyes, and weakness, treachery. He feared no man and heeded no opinion save the good of the Navy. He did not know or care how to compromise with political pressure. Whether it was the duke of Clarence or Mr Thomas Parlby who besought his favour for a friend or relative, his reply was the same:

> "for it is my fixed determination to fill all vacant offices with the most efficient men I can find, and to pay no regard to the recommendations of any person whatever, where the qualification of the candidate will not bear me out in the appointment. Meritorious clerks in office will have the first-fruits, and admirals' secretaries and pursers the next. As the Father of the Service I cannot travel out of this record, except in very extraordinary cases".[22]

St Vincent was undoubtedly a very great man, but he was not the best choice to be First Lord in 1801. The peace, which most people took for a breathing-space, he accepted at face value and ruthlessly ran down the fleet. He despised the work of the Navy Board as "dull insipid business, fit for Scotch pack-horses", and his reaction was not to reform, but to ignore it, virtually withdrawing all co-operation.

In 1802 he and his new Board went on a visitation of the dockyards.

Hugh Childers as First Lord *National Portrait Gallery*

The Admiralty from Whitehall in 1775, with Lord Kinnoul's house beyond. The engraver has embellished Nash's screen with statuary. *National Maritime Museum*

Nearly the same view in 1818. Note the semaphore telegraph and the hut for its operators erected on the roof.
Guildhall Library

The Board Room about 1800, by Pugin, with the figures added by Rowlandson. The First Lord sits at the near end of the table, with the Lords on either side and the Secretary at the far end. Beside him stands the Reader, and above his head is the tell-tale from the wind vane. Above the fireplace are rolled charts.

National Maritime Museum

The Board Room in 1934. The table now has a piece cut from the end, and the tell-tale has been moved over the fireplace, but otherwise little has changed. *G.L.C. Photograph Library*

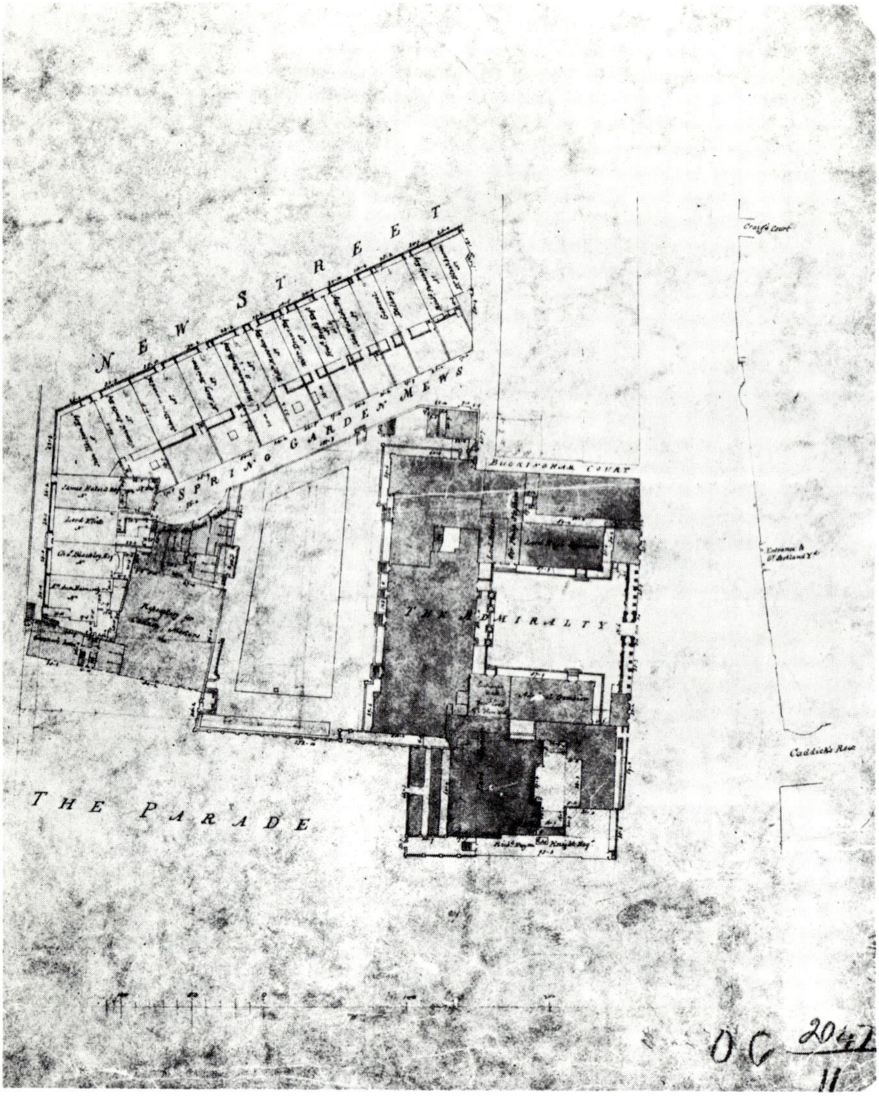

A plan of the Admiralty in about 1797. Besides Admiralty House, marked with Lord Spencer's name, much of the Admiralty building is taken up with the residences for the Lords. The First Lord's stables lie at the foot of the garden, giving onto Spring Gardens Mews. One of the householders in New Street is Mr Marsden, the Second Secretary. *Public Record Office, Work 30/477*

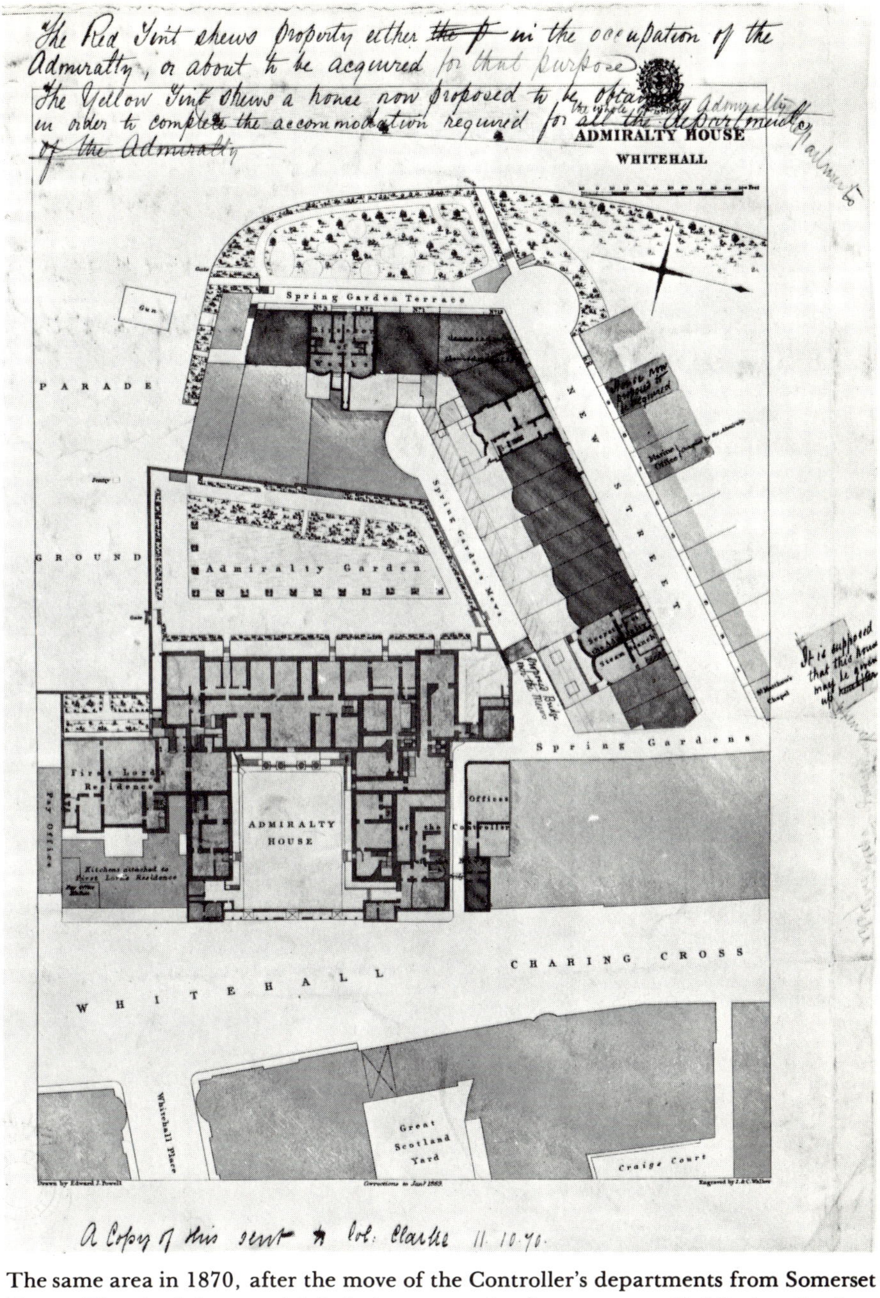

The same area in 1870, after the move of the Controller's departments from Somerset House. The shaded area of Admiralty occupation has now engulfed Spring Gardens Terrace, much of New Street, and parts of Spring Gardens.

Public Record Office, ADM 140/1115

The New Buildings from the Horse Guards Parade, soon after their completion *G.L.C. Photograph Library*

There he found that during the war wages had been inflated by fictitious piece-work. Previous Boards had known and accepted this as the only way to keep the shipwrights in the dockyards in a time of inflation when private shipyards could pay much higher wages. St Vincent treated it as straightforward corruption, and when the enraged workmen pelted him with mud, it only stiffened his resolution, if that were possible: "Burning with indignation at these misdeeds of persons who happily chanced to be the nominees of his political opponents", he declared open war on the Navy Board and all its works, and for his attack chose a familiar weapon. In December 1802, at the motion of Captain Markham, junior naval lord, Parliament established a Commission of Naval Enquiry to delve into the abuses of the system. *The Times* described it as a new Board of Control, intended as the Admiralty's means of controlling the Navy Board and the other subordinate bodies.[23]

It may be that a prolonged period of peace would have allowed this new Commission, partisan though it was, to reform the Navy Board, which was undoubtedly ill-organized to cope with the overwhelming business of a great war, and whose relations with the Admiralty had not for half a century been either easy or assured. In fact, in May 1803, less than fourteen months after the signature of the Peace of Amiens, Britain and France were again at war. Neither the Navy nor Addington's ministry was ready to face it; within a year Pitt was back as Prime Minister, and St Vincent's brief and unfortunate tenure of the First Lordship was over. He left two legacies which were to have a permanent effect. Firstly, it became an article of faith among those of his politics that the civil branch of the Navy was indeed rotten to the core, that the authority of the state and the efficiency of the Navy demanded that the Navy Board be reduced, absorbed or abolished. Secondly, the Commission of Naval Enquiry continued its work, producing a series of reports each faithfully reflecting the prejudices of its creator, embarrassing the government and delighting its opponents.[24]

In this difficulty Pitt and his new First Lord, viscount Melville, bethought themselves of an old acquaintance. Melville needed advice on naval policy, and had a kinsman who might provide it; Pitt needed an antidote to St Vincent's Commission, and had a protégé fit to produce one. In these circumstances Sir Charles Middleton returned once more to naval administration, as unofficial adviser to the First Lord, and chairman of the Commission for Revising and Digesting the Civil Affairs of the Navy, intended "as fire drives out fire", to neutralise the Commission of Naval Enquiry by proposing new and different reforms.[25]

The administration of the Navy, simultaneously scrutinized and interfered with by two warring Commissions, was now in a state of Gilbertian complexity, but there was worse to come. The Tenth Report of the Commission of Naval Enquiry, published in February 1805, showed that a late Paymaster of the Navy had speculated in public money, apparently with the connivance of his master the Treasurer of the Navy. The Treasurer in question was Lord Melville, who was obliged hurriedly to resign his seat and prepare to defend himself against impeachment.[26]

In the spring of 1805 the state of the naval war demanded a new first Lord at once, and demanded a man of ability, whatever his political demerits. Thus it was that Sir Charles Middleton, newly ennobled as Lord Barham, finally at the age of seventy-nine attained the supreme command of the Navy which he had so long desired. The war at sea was approaching its climax in the great campaign of Trafalgar. Six British squadrons were involved in operations spread over an area from the West Indies to the Channel, and these were only some of the squadrons at sea throughout the world. In order to co-ordinate all these far-distant ships, to articulate and unify a common strategy, the Admiralty had gradually become a centre of operational command. The number and complexity of the orders to be sent to so many ships in so many places, the volume of information received from the Admiralty's excellent intelligence system, had long exceeded the capacity of any one man, either commander at sea or First Lord at home, to comprehend. Once a single order from a Secretary of State could pass the Admiralty by and send a single fleet to sea upon whose commander everything depended. If Whitehall did try to interfere, as with Lord Torrington in 1690, the results were often disastrous. Now the scale of the war at sea was far beyond the control of any flag officer. Not only grand strategy, but such routine matters as trade protection, were conducted on a scale unheard of in previous wars. In

1792 more than thirteen thousand British ships entered and cleared home ports; by the Convoy Act of 1798 almost all of them were obliged to sail under escort. In the early years of the new century Baltic convoys of a thousand sail or more left fortnightly.[27]

The demands of war on this scale gave the Admiralty a rôle in operational command which it had never had before. To it came all despatches and information, from it flowed a constant stream of orders. The shutters of the telegraph on the roof could carry a signal to Spithead in three minutes, night or day in clear weather, and other lines ran to Plymouth, Deal, Sheerness and Harwich. A large fleet of swift schooners and cutters maintained communication with the fleets at sea.

This new function as a centre of operational command gave the Board a new importance. St Vincent had seen no use for junior naval lords, so little need was there for professional (or any other) abilities save in the First Lord. This new responsibility demanded sea officers of capacity ("I assure you the duty of the sea lords," wrote Barham, "will not bear an idle Lord to be one of them") and some division of duties among them. Barham therefore delegated the daily management of Admiralty affairs to them, reserving to himself "the general superintendence and arrangement of the whole", which included the direction of grand strategy. He understood and gave effect to the necessity of dividing daily administration from high policy if policy were not to be crowded out. Unhappily, the understanding died with him, and the want of it was to go far to cripple the Admiralty for more than a century.[28]

The Admiralty Office which transacted the daily business of the Board was by the last decades of the century very well settled in its character and methods. The manoeuvres of politicians, the quarrels of Comptrollers and First Lords, even the enquiries of Commissions and Committees, affected it relatively little. It had in a high degree all the respect for the proper channels, for seniority and establishment, of any settled and ordered administration. The attack of the 1797 Committee on its way of life was parried with disdainful ease. It expected and received a high standard of service from its officials. "The clerks to be informed," Barham noted, "that I expect an immediate reply to such minutes as come from me if the nature of them will admit of it; and where any unnecessary delay happens I shall expect to hear the reasons in writing." Its new operational rôle imposed very heavy demands. The clerks could be kept up until two in the morning copying urgent orders by lamplight. At least one had to be on duty all night. So it was that when Captain Lapenotière of the *Pickle* schooner clattered into the courtyard in the early hours of 6th November 1805 it was Mr Marsden the Second Secretary who received him, and went to wake old Lord Barham with his momentous news. "Sir," he said, drawing aside the bed curtains, "we have won a great victory, but we have lost Lord Nelson."[29]

Barham was sleeping in the new Admiralty House, built in 1786 on a site on the Horse Guards side of the Office obtained by the purchase and demolition of Lord Kinnoul's house, to provide a residence for the First Lord, who could no longer be allowed to be out of reach of the Admiralty even by night. It had the additional merit of providing room for official entertainment, so that no more dinners were served in the cramped splendour of the Board Room, with the Gibbons carving and the weather-vane over the fireplace.[30]

The Secretary of the Admiralty under Barham, Sir Evan Nepean, and his deputy and successor William Marsden, were worthy heirs of the Secretaries of the eighteenth century. In the opinion of that unsparing judge St Vincent, Nepean had made "his way to the first employments by superior talents for business, unremitting diligence, and integrity". Marsden was a distinguished orientalist, the historian of Sumatra, translator of Marco Polo, first lexicographer of Malay. One or other of them opened and read every letter that arrived in the Admiralty, and saw it answered and filed by the evening of the same day. The Office developed a unique and remarkedly effective system of registering its papers, the "Admiralty Digest", whose massive volumes (weighing upwards of ninety pounds each in their original form) running in unbroken series throughout the nineteenth and twentieth centuries, stand as an impressive tribute to the order and method of the Admiralty Office.[31]

As the Great War (as it was always known until a greater came to usurp the title) drew to its close, the Admiralty was securely established in the body politic. It was still very small—fifty-five in 1880, swollen by war, when the civil service as a whole exceeded sixteen thousand—

but it was remarkably efficient, it had reformed its internal management earlier and more thoroughly (albeit more idiosyncratically) than most other departments, and its new rôle of operational command made it almost impossible to ignore the Board or the Office as had been done before.[32] Nevertheless, the naval administration as a whole was not in a happy state. Once installed in supreme power, Barham had had no further interest in strengthening the Navy Board by reform, and it remained ill-adapted for the burdens of modern war. The two boards no longer liked or trusted one another, and were prepared to take offence over such trifling matters as the relative pay of the Admiralty Library cat and the Bill Office cat (an employee of the Navy Board). It had become an article of faith among the Whigs that the only thing to be done with the Navy Board was to abolish it out of hand. For the Tories, on the other hand, it had become the temple of all that was ancient and right in the administration of the Navy. For each of them, the merits of the old system in theory, and its defects in practice, were obscured by preconceived ideas. The position was neither stable nor satisfactory. It was certain the Whigs would change it if they had the chance, but they had little positive idea of what to put in its place. The virtues of one system or another had become almost entirely a political question, expressed in ideological or even moral terms, of personal responsibility and accountability. The control of the Admiralty by Parliament, and of the Navy Board by the Admiralty, concerned statesmen far more than the management of the Navy by either. It was curious legacy of a long and desperate war, in which the safety of the kingdom had depended chiefly on the Navy, that the real issues of how best to administer it hardly interested the leaders of society, and the fate of the Admiralty and the Navy Board was to be settled by considerations connected only distantly, if at all, with their real functions.[33]

NOTES

1 Laughton, *Barham MSS* II, 66.
2 Mackesy, 4-5.
3 Mackesy, 8, 11. Martelli, *Jemmy Twitchem*, 220-223. Namier, 41.
4 Aspinall-Oglander, 220. Binney, *British Public Finance*, 8.
5 Parris, *Constitutional Bureaucracy*, 28, 40-42. Baugh, *BNA*, 465.

6 Martelli, 86, 122-123, 222-223, 235. Broomfield, MM LI, 8. Mackesy, 19-20.
7 Martelli, 26, 86, 126.
8 Martelli, 18, 34, 83-85, 118. Knight, MM LVII, 175. Barnes and Owen, *Sandwich MSS* IV, 282-283. Mackesy, 19-21.
9 M. K. Barritt, "The Navy and the Clyde in the American War 1777-1783" MM LV, 40. Syrett, *Shipping & the American War,* 10, 13, 244, 246. Condon, MM XLVIII, 69-70, 79.
10 Syrett, 2, 35. Mackesy, 19-21, 379. Martelli, 183. Barnes and Owen, IV, 5.
11 Mackesy, 19. Crimmin, MM LIII, 63. Finer, PA XXX, 349. Binney, 140-145.
12 Knight, MM LVII, 175, 188. Broomfield, MM LI, 7-11. Mackesy, 237-245. Barnes and Owen, IV, 299-300.
13 Murray, VI, 336. Mackesy, 163. Knight, MM LVII, 176. Laughton, I, viii-xxiv. Corbett, *Spencer MSS* I, 6.
14 Knight, MM LVII, 175. Syrett, 7. Laughton, II, 5, 7, 10. Martelli, 25, 73.
15 Syrett, 23. Mackesy, 164-165, 485.
16 Murray, VI, 335. Knight, MM LVII, 176, 186.
17 Pool, MM L, 162-164. Binney, 7-14. Crimmin, MM LV, 299. Barnes and Owen, IV, 183, 232-233, 272, 287. Murray, VI, 337. Condon, MM XLVIII, 70.
18 Murray, VI, 338. Binney, 17.
19 Condon, MM XLVIII, 78-79. Murray, VI, 339-341. Glover, *Britain at Bay,* 35. Laughton, I, xiv; II, 315.
20 Laughton, II, 421. Murray, VI, 339-341. Corbett, I, xi-xii, 183.
21 Crimmin, MM LV, 299-309.
22 Smith, *St. Vincent MSS* I, 12, 302-303. Pool, MM L, 166. Murray, VI, 342-344. Richmond, *Spencer MSS* IV, 4.
23 Pool, MM L, 167, 172. Murray, VI, 343-344. Lloyd, *Mr. Barrow,* 72-73. Richmond, IV. 3-4. Smith, *St. Vincent* I, 8-18.
24 Smith, *St. Vincent* I, 67. Murray, VI, 344. Pool, MM LIV, 209-210.
25 Phillips, MM LXIV, 218. Murray, VI, 344-345. Lloyd, *Mr Barrow,* 80.
26 Holden Furber, *Henry Dundas, First Viscount Melville, 1742-1811* (London, 1931), 149. Murray, VI, 345.
27 Phillips, MM LXIV, 219-220. Glover, 55-76. Crowhurst, *Defence of Trade,* 70-74.
28 Geoffrey Wilson, *The Old Telegraphs* (Chichester, 1976), 13-14. Phillips, MM LXIV, 222-224.
29 Syrett, 6-8. Crimmin, MM LV, 303-309. Phillips, MM LXIV, 229. Mackesy, 379. Smith, *St. Vincent* I, 62. Lloyd, *Mr. Barrow,* 84.
30 Smith, MM IX, 278.
31 Richmond, IV, 8. Smith, *St Vincent* I, 368-369. Lloyd, *Mr. Barrow,* 76-78, 108. Pugh, "Early History of the Admiralty Record Office".
32 Sainty, 103-104. Finer, PA XXX, 346. Crimmin, MM LV, 309.
33 Murray, VI, 346, 349. Phillips, MM LXIV, 221. Parry, *Parry,* 10. Tunstall, "Imperial Defence", 807-811.

CHAPTER SIX

BOARDS OF ADMIRALTY 1815-1827

First Lord:

25th March 1812	Robert Dundas, Viscount Melville

First Naval Lords:

23rd October 1813	Sir Joseph Yorke
2nd April 1818	Sir Graham Moore
13th March 1820	Sir William Johnstone Hope

First Secretary:

12th October 1809	John Wilson Croker

Second Secretary:

9th April 1807	John Barrow

LORD ADMIRAL 1827-1828

2nd May 1827	William, Duke of Clarence

Senior Members of the Lord Admiral's Council:*

2nd May 1827	Sir William Johnstone Hope
12th March 1828	Sir George Cockburn

Second Secretary:

9th April 1807	John Barrow

BOARDS OF ADMIRALTY 1828-1868

First Lords:

19th September 1828	Robert Dundas, Viscount Melville
25th November 1830	Sir James Graham
11th June 1834	George Eden, Lord Auckland
23rd December 1834	Thomas, Earl de Grey
25th April 1835	George Eden, Lord Auckland
19th September 1835	Gilbert Elliot, Earl of Minto
8th September 1841	Thomas Hamilton, Earl of Haddington
13th January 1846	Edward Law, Earl of Ellenborough
13th July 1846	George Eden, Earl of Auckland
18th January 1849	Sir Francis Baring
2nd March 1852	Algernon Percy, Duke of Northumberland
5th January 1853	Sir James Graham
8th March 1855	Sir Charles Wood

*Naval members in both cases

8th March 1858	Sir John Pakington
28th June 1859	Edward Seymour, Duke of Somerset
13th July 1866	Sir John Pakington
8th March 1867	Henry Lowry Corry

First Naval Lords:

19th September 1828	Sir George Cockburn
25th November 1830	Sir Thomas Hardy
1st August 1834	George Dundas
1st November 1834	Charles Adam
23rd December 1834	Sir George Cockburn
25th April 1835	Sir Charles Adam
8th September 1841	Sir George Cockburn
13th July 1846	Sir William Parker
24th July 1846	Sir Charles Adam
20th July 1847	James Deans Dundas
13th February 1852	Maurice Berkeley
2nd March 1852	Hyde Parker
3rd June 1854	Maurice Berkeley
24th November 1857	Sir Richard Saunders Dundas
8th March 1858	William Martin
28th June 1859	Sir Richard Saunders Dundas
15th June 1861	Sir Frederick Grey
13th July 1866	Sir Alexander Milne

Second Secretaries:

9th April 1807	Sir John Barrow
28th January 1845	William Baillie Hamilton
22nd May 1855	Thomas Phinn
7th May 1857	William Romaine

CHAPTER SIX

Unity and Simplicity

"If I hear people saying that something must be done, I know that they contemplate doing something damn silly."

attributed to Lord Melbourne

THE end of the Great War against France was the beginning of an era in British history which was to change the face of the nation out of all recognition, and the Navy likewise. Never before, however, had the Navy and the nation had less in common. For three centuries the Service had been increasingly valuable to, and valued by, the leaders of the country in peace and war; it had generally been the largest government employer and the most expensive government service; it had saved the state and made and unmade dynasties. Since Queen Elizabeth's reign no generation of sea officers had grown old in service without the experience of battle against the fleets of the enemy, and no ministry had neglected to keep up a fleet which almost always exceeded that of powers much greater and stronger than England. The country depended for its prosperity on a powerful Navy, and the prosperous part of the nation knew it.

All this was to change with remarkable swiftness. The nineteenth century was the age in which the Navy and the nation grew further apart than ever before, in which the nation became the mightiest in the world, and the fleet shrank to a smaller size, both absolutely and relative to foreign powers, than at any time since the reign of James I. In this era of the Pax Britannica both statesmen and sea officers ceased to know, and in many cases to care, what the Navy existed for. As the country's influence expanded, the Navy's intellectual horizons contracted. The mighty force which had stood alone as the last coherent opposition to Napoleon was content to chase dhows and burn villages in the obscure and unhealthy backwaters of the world. The Royal Navy had gained an empire, and lost a rôle.

The Tory government which was in power when the Peace of Vienna was signed, and remained until 1830, could not reasonably have been accused of radical sympathies, but it was not unaffected by the climate of the times. A new spirit was abroad in the land, a spirit of morality and responsibility. Bentham's formula of individual responsibility as the key to honesty and efficiency was on all lips. Boards were no more than a mechanism for dissipating responsibility; behind their bland exterior, sloth and incapacity slumbered undisturbed, peculation and favouritism flourished unchecked. The profligacy of government was both the cause and the effect of the corruption of civil society, as the patronage of the state built, preserved and sheltered within an edifice of privilege from which all its inmates benefited, and only the public suffered. For the Whigs, Radicals and Evangelicals who pressed the new ideas with varying emphasis and enthusiasm, this was in large measure a moral crusade for freedom and honesty. The efficiency of state administration was not the primary object of their attention; it was assumed to flow automatically from right measures, rightly applied. The new currents of thought were not so much concerned with the objects of administration as with the means of attaining them; it mattered chiefly that the state should conduct its affairs in a plainly moral fashion, and from a morally sound system would necessarily proceed efficiency and policy.[1]

The Tory government did not altogether care for these sentiments, but it could not afford to ignore them. At the conclusion of peace the Navy was swiftly and ruthlessly reduced. In 1812 there had been 543 ships in commission, manned by 130,000 officers and men. In five years there were but 20,000 left. Of ninety-eight sail of the line, thirteen remained. A shrunken force shrank in political standing. Within living memory a First Lord had dominated the Cabinet and directed the policy of a nation at war; now the Board was presided over by a succession of uninspiring mediocrities. In the opinion of one well-placed (albeit partisan) observer, only one First Lord in half a century enjoyed real Cabinet support. The second viscount Melville, First Lord almost continuously from 1812 to 1830, was described by an enthusiastic fellow Scot as "judicious, clairvoyant and uncommonly soundheaded, like his father", and by a colleague as a "most amiable and worthy man, and very good at business". In truth, he seems to have possessed only moderate talents, and his clairvoyance did not prevent him appointing a second captain to a ship he had already given away once.[2]

Melville's long period in office was interrupted in 1827 by a bizarre constitutional experiment. Canning's government found it politically expedient to give the duke of Clarence something to do by creating him Lord High Admiral. Clarence was by no means a fool, and had made quite a competent post-captain, but no one credited him with administrative ability, and it was taken for granted that the Board would continue to function as before under the guise of the Lord Admiral's Council. Unfortunately the Duke envisaged a more active rôle for himself, and not only in giving dinner parties, of which he was very fond. He had a generous spirit, especially with public money, and he began eagerly to improve the Navy and the lot of its officers and men. An enthusiastic reformer, ignorant and careless of restraints both practical and financial, was not at all what the ministry had had in mind, and in September 1828 the duke of Wellington's government restored the Board and relegated the duke of Clarence once more to Bushey. This brief interlude, the last occasion when a Lord Admiral assumed his ancient privileges and hoisted his flag at sea, in reality only emphasized that the Board of Admiralty had become the permanent feature of the constitution, and the Lord Admiral an aberration. Whereas the Admiralty Act of 1690 had vested all the Admiral's powers in the Board, the Admiralty Act of 1827, by a curious and significant reversal, vested all the Lords Commissioners' powers in the Admiral.[3]

When First Lords were not expected to be men of great weight or ability, the junior lords were naturally less so. Palmerston, who sat at the Board for two years, described his duties as "passing a couple of hours in the Board Room doing little or nothing", and one First Lord quoted in this connection Canning's description of the business of a junior lord of the Treasury "to make a House, to keep a House, and to cheer the Minister".[4]

It was difficult to find sea officers politically and professionally (to say nothing of physically) fit to be senior naval lord. All promotion above captain's rank was still by seniority, and the enormous flag lists of the war meant that officers grew old reaching high rank, and went seldom to sea. In 1843 the average age of the full admirals was seventy-six, the youngest rear-admiral was fifty-three, and the three hundred senior captains in 1845 were on average over sixty. The young rear-admiral was Sir Richard Dundas, son of the second Lord Melville, a captain at twenty-two. When he finally gained his flag after more than thirty years' waiting he lamented, "It has come too late; had I been made an admiral ten years ago there was nothing I then felt I could not do, but now I have had forty years' service taken out of me". Yet he was young and lucky. In the 1840s an officer of seventy-one, who had not been at sea for thirty years, was made Commander-in-Chief in the West Indies. Another paid off a frigate in 1826, and did not go to sea again until he hoisted his flag as Vice-Admiral and Commander-in-Chief at the Nore twenty-eight years later.[5]

The Boards of the early years of peace were not in general made up of men of calibre. The ministries' principles prevented them from reforming naval administration, but did not oblige them to place any trust in it. In one respect, however, the spirit of reform did achieve an important change. Hitherto the Secretary of the Admiralty had combined both political and administrative duties, as had the Second Secretary, a deputy appointed in time of war only. The combination had become highly offensive, and a division of responsibility came about. John Wilson Croker was First Secretary from 1809 to 1830, and Sir John Barrow Second Secretary from 1804 to 1806, and from 1807 to 1845. By the end of their service the character of their offices had become clearly distinct. Croker was an extreme conservative in politics, able, ambitious, arrogant and autocratic. He kept a tight control on the business of the office, opening every letter with his own hand. In the words of an admittedly hostile observer, he was "opposed to everything in the shape of reform and improvement"; he was certainly opposed to anything in the shape of expense. As a politician and writer as well as Secretary, his influence was considerable. As a delegate to the Congress of Vienna in 1815, he was empowered to issue orders directly to H.M. Ships as though he had been the Board personified.[6]

Barrow, too, was a man of wide influence, but in different spheres. He was an authority on China and South Africa, founder of the Royal Geographical Society, adviser to John Murray and leading contributor to the *Quarterly Review,* father of Arctic exploration. A poor boy from Lancashire who had risen by his own ability, a "wise and friendly administrator" who in forty years served four sovereigns, thirteen ministries, forty Boards and a Lord Admiral, Barrow may well be considered the archetype of the Permanent Secretary. From the day when Croker left office with Wellington's ministry in 1830, the first Secretary of the Admiralty to be dismissed on unequivocally political grounds since James Southerne in 1694, and Barrow remained, the distinction was clear between the First Secretary, the Parliamentary or Financial Secretary as he came to be known, and the Second, or Permanent Secretary; the first a junior minister and a minor politician, the second the real heir to Pepys as permanent head of the naval administration, and in common parlance simply "the Secretary".[7]

This divorce was one expression of the fact that the Admiralty's political influence was declining fast. Even after the Reform Act of 1832 the Board had some political patronage to dispose of, but it was increasingly felt to be more of a nuisance than an asset, and the days when Prime Ministers needed to court Secretaries of the Admiralty—or First Lords—were gone. Fewer officers had seats in Parliament, so there was less influence to employ, and the First Secretary defended the ministry's naval policy in the House.[8]

The Boards of the 1820s met together for the collective dispatch of business. The First Lord, reduced in stature, no longer decided vital questions with his Cabinet colleagues beforehand, for there were few vital questions to be decided about the Navy. A clerk appointed for the duty read each letter aloud to the Board, and the Board took a collective decision upon it. The junior lords had no rooms of their own, and all their affairs had to be transacted at the Board. Attentive or distracted, busy or idle, asleep or awake, eating luncheon or reading the newspapers, they passed their whole service at the Admiralty around the smooth mahogany of the Board Room table. Barham's division of responsibility was almost forgotten. At a time when board management elsewhere in government had become fictional, the weakness of the First Lords who had once dominated their Boards without question was making the Admiralty more genuinely collective than ever before.[9]

In 1830 Grey's Liberal administration, with the pent-up enthusiasm of men who had fretted most of their adult lifetimes under a succession of Tory governments, set out to work sweeping changes in the constitution, not least by the great Reform Act of 1832. Besides this the Admiralty Act of the same year was relatively unimportant, but it was nevertheless the most decisive single constitutional change ever made in the administration of the Navy. When Grey's government came to power in 1830, the Admiralty and the Navy Board were substantially unchanged in structure. Semi-autonomous bodies like the Navy Board embodied all that the new ministry distrusted. The First Lord, Sir James Graham, was a young and inexperienced politician, whose service on the committee which had planned the Reform Bill had sufficiently impressed Grey to gain him a Cabinet post. Everyone, including Graham himself, was amazed to find him there, but no-one could be in any doubt that he came with a mandate to reform. His first instinct, and his first political duty, was to reduce spending, and the Navy Board was his first target. Its abolition would secure "a just division of labour, an undivided control and a due responsibility on the one hand, and, on the other, that unity and simplicity which he held to be the very essence and life of public business". By 1832 one hint of how that might be achieved was to hand. Almost as soon as he had arrived at the Admiralty Graham had quarrelled with Sir Thomas Byam Martin, the Comptroller, an aged and reactionary Tory, and on his dismissal one of the Lords of the Admiralty was temporarily put in charge of the Navy Board. In spite of this precedent, it does not seem that Graham had any developed ideas of how to achieve his desired objects of economy and individual responsibility. It was Sir John Barrow who suggested that each Lord Commissioner be made responsible for a part of the administrative business transacted by the subordinate boards.[10]

This was the model adopted in the new Act. In place of the old junior boards there were now five "Principal Officers": the Accountant-General, Storekeeper-General, Comptroller of Victualling, Physician and Surveyor. Each was responsible for the affairs of a "branch" of the administration to one of the Lords Commissioners. Thus that ancient and redoubtable body the Navy Board met its end, and the Admiralty at last became in reality the supreme governor and director of the affairs of the Navy.

By these changes Graham was able to reduce the Estimates by £1,200,000 to £4,650,000. Twelve Commissioners, sixty-one superior and thirty-seven inferior dockyard officers were dismissed, and over a hundred clerks. The victualling organization and the packet service were investigated, salaries cut, clerks' working hours increased, sailors' meat rations reduced. A system of internal audit was introduced, anticipating and providing the model for the Exchequer and Audit Act of 1866.[11]

Like so many revolutionaries, Graham was in social matters an instinctive conservative. He wished to reform the Admiralty to its pristine efficiency, not to subvert or undermine the naval administration. He intended that the Lords Commissioners should be both individually responsible for their branches, and yet perfectly informed of one another's activities. It was the practice at the Board under Graham for the responsible Lord to read the papers concerning his branch, get up the previous correspondence ("former" was the Admiralty term) and make any necessary minutes before the Board meeting, at which Mr Briggs, the Reader to the Board, read the letter aloud for it to be discussed by the Board as a whole, and some decision come to.[12]

Graham intended that the Board should provide a mechanism for mutual discussion and information without impairing individual responsibility. It is possible that the scheme might have worked if the volume of business had remained very small, but it did not. In Barrow's time the number of letters passing through the hands of the Secretary every year increased from 25,402 to 47,866. Each Lord was now responsible for a great department, the management of which had formerly been confided to one or more members of the Navy Board, and yet his former duties at the Admiralty Board had not evaporated. The burden was very great, and growing all the time. A relentless flow of administrative questions, many of them very detailed, came before the Board and claimed its attention. The larger questions of policy and strategy which the First Lord and his principal naval adviser were especially charged with were at first neglected, and then forgotten. "The departmental duties entailed upon the First Sea Lord were so arduous and multifarious that it was with difficulty that he could get through the daily routine of office work, much less find time for the careful consideration of those grave and important questions of national defence".[13]

Worse, from Graham's point of view, the Board suffered more than before from the ills that boards, in Whig eyes, were heir to. Responsibility for the decisions taken around the Board Room table became even more elusive, and yet co-ordination of the different branches, which had no links except at the top, became less rather than more effective.[14]

For the moment, however, the defects of Graham's scheme were not obvious. He had sharply reduced the Estimates, and economy, in the Whig view, naturally indicated, if it was not actually identical with, greater efficiency. Graham enjoyed the support of the Cabinet and the assistance, as First Naval Lord, of Sir Thomas Masterman Hardy, Nelson's old flag-captain, who was undoubtedly the finest sea officer to reach the Admiralty in the nineteenth century. In an age when all admirals were elderly, and almost all were conservative in the extreme, Hardy's motto was "happen what will, England's duty is to take and keep the lead". He believed strongly in scientific analysis as a basis for policy, and looked forward to fundamental changes in naval warfare which few of his contemporaries foresaw, let alone welcomed. This wise and prudent reformer was not the least of the benefits which Graham's successors had cause to envy him.[15]

First Lords and First Naval Lords in the years from the Admiralty Act to the outbreak of the Crimean War were with few exceptions men outranked in government, and superannuated in service. Lord Auckland who was First Lord in 1834, in 1835, and again from 1846 to his death in 1849, was a talented administrator, justly popular in the Admiralty and the Navy, but his complete inability to speak in public disqualified him from high office. Sir Charles Adam who served seven years as senior naval adviser to Auckland and Lord Minto was a very poor man of business, and his handwriting was illegible even to himself. Minto was a dull and uninspiring leader, and the worthy Lord Haddington was largely dominated by his Senior Naval Lord. Sir Francis Baring was competent, but his failure as Chancellor of the Exchequer had not improved his standing in government. The duke of Northumberland, who served a single unfortunate year in 1852-1853, was the first naval officer to head the Board since Barham, but had not been to sea for nearly forty years, and was quite destitute of political standing or professional ability. Sir Charles Wood, First Lord from 1855 to 1858 was a man of great charm and capacity, but like the others, he was a politician of the second rank. The unhappy career of Lord Ellenborough, who "quitted office in July 1846 a frustrated and disgruntled man", less than six months after coming to the Admiralty full of energy and enthusiasm to revive and reform the Service, admirably illustrates the weakness of a First Lord without powerful allies, and an enthusiasm for naval affairs which Victorian Cabinets hardly ever possessed.[16]

Of the Senior Naval Lords of the period, only Sir George Cockburn, who sat on fifteen Boards and the Lord Admiral's Council, dominating the Admiralty in Haddington's time, requires mention. A ruthless, domineering, energetic man, "he seemed to live in the past, and was impressed with the conviction that everything that had been done was right; that what was being done was questionable, and every step in advance was fraught with danger". Yet Cockburn's "considerable talents were not wholly devoted to the defence of lost causes"; he was firmly in favour of promoting men young rather than relying on ill and elderly men like himself, kept on for want of able successors. The man who had burnt Washington in 1814 was seldom gentle with opponents, but he had great ability and knew how to use it.[17]

The Boards of the 1840s and 1850s were faced with many novel and difficult problems. Technical progress was beginning to affect the Navy. Graham wearily remarked of his Surveyor, "Except on matters of religion, I do not know of any difference of opinion which has been attended with so much bitterness—so much anger—so much resentment, as the merits of Sir W. Symonds and the virtues of his ships". One question came to dominate the material changes of the Navy; the question of steam. The Boards of Admiralty of those days have been caricatured as blinkered reactionaries, "opposed to everything in the shape of reform and improvement". One pronouncement in particular has often been quoted; "Their Lordships feel it their bounden duty to discourage to the utmost of their ability the introduction of steam vessels, as they consider that the introduction of steam is calculated to strike a fatal blow at the naval supremacy of the Empire". In fact, in the 1820s when this and similar statements were made, they represented an eminently sensible position. Steam vessels were not yet reliable sea-going ships, let alone warships, and until some other power took them up, there was every reason for a prudent Board to discourage them. Once the steamer began to be a useful addition to the fleet, successive Boards took it seriously, first as an auxiliary, and in time as a fighting ship. In 1835 the first Chief Engineer and Inspector of Machinery was appointed, at a Master Shipwright's salary, and the distinguished Arctic explorer Sir Edward Parry, who became first Comptroller of Steam Machinery in 1837, applied his great talents to improving engines and engineering, raising the status of engineers, and introducing the screw. There were reactionary opponents of steam—Sir William Symonds was one—but even such conservative figures as Byam Martin and Cockburn appreciated its importance, and Graham and Hardy, within two months of taking office, had ordered four of the largest and most powerful steamers in the world.[18]

It is arguable that the Admiralty's approach to the introduction of steam was considerably more far-sighted than that of private ship-owners, and that it proved surprisingly good at adapting to new technologies, at least at the relatively slow rate of change up to the 1860s. It was a characteristic opinion of the times that corporate bodies, especially government bodies, were of their nature reactionary. The heroes of the Victorian age were the entrepreneurs, especially the engineers. These were the men who made themselves wealthy and the country great by advancing the frontiers of technology, not a board of elderly admirals and second-rate politicians. Moreover the great engineers were often gifted publicists. The men who caught the public's attention with their denunciations were frequently those who had suffered at the Admiralty's hands rejection of some favourite (and potentially lucrative) proposal. The pages of the Admiralty Digest headed "Inventions and Visionary Suggestions" grew more numerous every year, as the number of eager inventors increased. Novel types of armour were a popular favourite, such as india-rubber or springs (so that the shot would bounce off), canvas, gutta-percha, papier-mâché and old boots. One may therefore read with some scepticism the partisan complaints even of so great an engineer as Brunel:

> "They have an extraordinary supply of cold water and capacious and heavy extinguishers, but I was prepared for and proof against

such coarse offensive measures. But they have an unlimited supply of some *negative* principle, which seems to absorb and eliminate everything that approaches them . . . it is a curious and puzzling phenomena [*sic*], but in my experience it has always attended every contact with the Admiralty".[19]

Nevertheless, the Royal Navy in the 1840s and 1850s was not deeply involved in the burgeoning life of a great industrial nation. It was by any standards extremely small, and heavily involved in distant waters. Though the 1840s were years in which the fear that "steam has bridged the Channel" were at their height, there were never as many as ten line of battleships available. When the 1844 crisis threatened war with France, the Mediterranean Fleet consisted only of a single ship, reinforced by four more only at the cost of leaving no battleships at all in commission in home waters. At the same time there were twenty-five or more vessels engaged in surveying. The Cabinet knew and cared little for the Navy. The Admiralty became a curiously parochial organization, increasingly bound up with routine administration. As late as the 1850s the Secretary, W. G. Romaine, opened and read every incoming letter himself. No concern was too detailed to be referred to the Board, or too technical to be decided by its members. Auckland once entered the Board Room to find Sir William Parker, the First Naval Lord, and Admiral Dundas, his junior colleague, sprawled over the table altering the lines of a ship's draught the Surveyor had just submitted. The working of the Admiralty Office, though still very efficient compared with other sections of the unreformed civil service, was undoubtedly slower than it had been in wartime. Auckland, a harsh but acute judge,considered that "the mode of transacting business in the office is such as to induce the belief that no mind can have been employed about it since the time of Pepys and James Duke of York".[20]

By the time of the Crimean War, when he was recalled as First Lord, even Sir James Graham was unhappy about the Admiralty. The habit of collective decision had gone so far that the authority of the First Lord over his Board was in some doubt. Personal responsibility, far from being fixed in 1832, was more elusive than ever. "So far from being an example to be followed," he said of the system he had himself designed, "it might on the whole be regarded as an example to be avoided." Though it was clear that during the war Graham and the First Naval Lord at times kept their colleagues in ignorance for the sake of secrecy, though Sir Frances Baring among other former First Lords was quite clear that "the Entire responsibility of the Navy rests upon the First Lord", the issue of who was really answerable to Parliament seemed to be more confused than ever. To the Whig Parliamentary committees which sought reason for the failures of the Crimean War nothing could have been more provoking. In 1861 the M.P. for Portsmouth moved that the Admiralty be replaced by a Ministry of Marine. A Select Committee of the House of Lords was appointed by Palmerston, including all four former First Lords in the House, "much to the anxiety of the champions of change, who foresaw that with so much weight aboard the ship was likely to sink before she reached port". They were right; the Committee never reported. Nevertheless there was plainly something wrong when the duke of Somerset, First Lord from 1859 to 1866, and a man not lacking in character, could speak of persuading his colleagues with "such influence as he may possess", and could not conceive of a First Lord overruling the Board — "a doctrine calculated to make First Lords of the eighteenth century turn in their graves". Not only Liberals were disquieted by the state of affairs in what, after the abolition of the Ordnance Board in 1855, remained the last of the seventeenth-century boards to have preserved any form of corporate structure. "The human memory," commented the duke of Somerset wearily in an anonymous pamphlet, "cannot recall the period when the department of the Admiralty was not the subject of accusation and complaint". [21]

In the public eye, the Admiralty might require reform, but it did not demand serious study. Cabinet discussion of naval affairs was invariably conducted on a plain of ignorance and unconcern only imaginable in an age when a serious military threat was hardly conceivable by most statesmen. The reform of the civil service was a far more pressing concern, and, characteristically, more for the benefit of the universities and public schools than for the state. "Admission into the Civil Service is indeed eagerly desired," wrote the Northcote-Trevelyan Report of 1854, "but it is for the unambitious and the indolent or incapable, that it is chiefly desired." Many government departments had not yet reached the state of efficiency of the Admiralty under Pepys. The War office "led an administrative life of exquisite confusion", which was held largely responsible for the disasters of the Crimean War.[22] More important even than civil service reform was financial control by Treasury and Parliament, which represented the quintessential element of mid-Victorian reform. Again the motive was not primarily greater efficiency but the moral desirability of a system in which nothing was spent but what had been voted for that purpose. There were thus more important things to do than reform the Admiralty, though it was generally agreed that reform was necessary.[23]

The weakness which the men of the 1860s saw in the Admiralty was that of a large and expensive department subject to very imperfect control by Parliament, by the Treasury, and by its own minister. In this they did not mistake, but they missed a more serious failing. The Boards of the 1860s were in charge of a ministry with a staff of over a thousand, to say nothing of the Navy itself, and they were not only responsible collectively for the whole, but individually for the parts. The burden of administration on each of the Lords, especially the Naval Lords, who were the only sea officers in their departments, and alone qualified to judge of any question, however trivial, which required professional knowledge, was great enough to drive out all consideration of general policy.[24] In the passage of thirty years, unnoticed by contemporaries in and out of the Service, the central direction of naval policy had almost evaporated. The Cabinet no longer cared enough to interfere, and the Admiralty for its part had been swallowed up by the duties, and the attitudes, of the Navy Board. The system was supportable so long as the Navy itself remained largely untouched by the technical changes which had overturned the social and economic fabric of nineteenth-century England, so long as it remained small, and so long as no great questions of naval policy demanded decision. By the 1860s all these conditions were about to pass away for ever.

NOTES

1 Pool, MMLIV, 210. Murray, VII, 458. Parris, 83-85. Finer, PA XXX, 329, 341.

2 Ritchie, *Admiralty Chart,* 101. Lloyd, *Mr. Barrow,* 89, 91. Bartlett, *Gt. Britain & Sea Power,* 4-5. Briggs, *Naval Administrations,* xxi. Jennings, *Croker MSS* I, 39. Parry, 10.

3 Murray, I, 27-28. Lloyd, *Mr. Barrow,* 94-96.

4 Parris, 125. Murray, VII, 459.

5 Bartlett, 6-8, 44-46. Briggs, 261-262.

6 Lloyd, *Mr. Barrow,* 75, 86-87. ADM 116/3453, memo. by W. G. Perrin. Jennings I, 20. Briggs, 6. Ritchie, 101. Parry, 124-127. Hamilton, *Naval Administration,* 39.

7 Parris, 137. Lloyd, *Mr. Barrow,* 9-11.

8 Bartlett, 298. ADM 116/3452 *loc. cit.*

9 ADM 116/3453 *loc. cit..* Lloyd, *Mr. Barrow,* 77. Finer, PA XXX, 347.

10 Bartlett, 9. Ward, *Graham,* 96-121, 126-128. Smith, MM XXXI, 154. Lloyd, *Mr. Barrow,* 99-100.

11 Murray, I, 28. Bartlett, 10. C. S. Parker, *Life and Letters of Sir James Graham* (London, 1907, 2 vols.) I, 147, 155. Finer, PA XXX, 351.

12 Ward, xiv-xv. Briggs, 38, 323.

13 Lloyd, *Mr. Barrow,* 103. Briggs, 241.

14 Lloyd, *Mr. Barrow,* 105. Murray, VII, 458-460.

15 Briggs, xxi, 15-17, 259, 294. Bartlett, 8, 52.

16 Bartlett, 182, 212, 222, 259-260, 273. Briggs, 57, 99-100, 118. Parry, 197.

17 Briggs, 6-11, 262. Bartlett, 6, 9, 222.

18 Bartlett, 202-209, 222-224. Briggs, 6. Parry, 197-217.

19 Bartlett, 219, 337. R. A. Buchanan & M. W. Doughty, "The Choice of Steam Engine Manufacturers by the Admiralty, 1822-1852" MM LXIV, 327.

20 Bartlett, 10n.2, 153-156. Briggs, 82, 157.

21 Murray, VII, 461-470. ADM 116/3453, quoting evidence given to 1861 Select Committee. *Naval Expenditure from 1860 to 1866* (London, 1867), 3.

22 For a specimen of a Cabinet discussion, see Christopher Howard and Peter Gordon, eds., "The Cabinet Journal of Dudley Ryder, Viscount Sandon" (BIHR Special Supplement Nno. 10, 1974), 50. Bartlett, 171. Hughes, PA XXXII, 27-29. Cd. 1713, quoted in PA XXXII, 2. Finer, PA XXX, 342. Murray, VII, 463, Sir Sam Fay, *The War Office at War* (London, 1937), 16. Johnson, *Defence by Committee,* 15.

23 Ashworth, EcHR 2° XXII, 496-497. Hughes, PA XXXII, 27-29.

24 Wright, *Treasury Control,* 181. Bartlett, 11. Lloyd, *Mr. Barrow,* 105. Murray, VII, 460-461. Rodger, MM LXI, 333.

CHAPTER SEVEN

BOARDS OF ADMIRALTY 1868-1904

First Lords:

18th December 1868	Hugh Childers
9th March 1871	George Goschen
4th March 1874	George Ward Hunt
14th August 1877	William Henry Smith
12th May 1880	Thomas Baring, Earl of Northbrook
1st July 1885	Lord George Hamilton
15th February 1886	George Robinson, Marquess of Ripon
9th August 1886	Lord George Hamilton
25th August 1892	John, Earl Spencer
6th July 1895	George Goschen
12th November 1900	William Palmer, Earl of Selborne

First Naval Lords:

18th December 1868	Sir Sydney Dacres
27th November 1872	Sir Alexander Milne
7th September 1876	Sir Hastings Yelverton
6th November 1877	George Wellesley
15th September 1879	Sir Astley Cooper Key
1st July 1885	Sir Arthur Hood
26th October 1889	Sir Richard Vesey Hamilton
28th September 1891	Sir Anthony Hoskins
1st November 1893	Sir Frederick Richards
14th August 1899	Lord Walter Kerr

Permanent Secretaries:

7th May 1857	William Romaine
29th June 1869	Vernon Lushington
	Robert Hall*
13th June 1882	George Tryon†
2nd April 1884	Sir Evan Macgregor

*From Lushington's retirement in June 1877 until Tryon's appointment, the office was technically abolished, but Admiral Hall, who was Naval Secretary 1872-1882, performed virtually identical duties.

†Tryon, the only serving naval officer ever to have been Secretary, was initially appointed to act *vice* R. G. C. Hamilton, Accountant-General of the Navy, who had just been chosen acting Under-Secretary at Dublin Castle; both appointments were later confirmed.

CHAPTER SEVEN

A Posthumous Revenge

"The Admiralty swallowed up the Navy Office, and the Navy Office swallowed up the function of the Admiralty. The successors of Anson and Barham became slaves of the lamp of administration and supply, much as if the kitchen was out of order and the mistress of the house was sent down to personally supervise the cook. The kitchen would no doubt be reformed, but the general direction of the house would suffer."

Captain A. C. Dewar[1]

FOR the second time in the century, the administration of the Navy was the subject of sharp criticism from the Liberals, and on virtually the same grounds as before. One of the largest and most expensive of government departments was apparently out of public control. It was making strenuous efforts to resist the novel and distasteful imposition of Treasury supervision, and its archaic board structure seemed designed on purpose to make it impossible to hold anyone responsible for anything. It has to be emphasized that neither party was interested in the "remote, complex and uninteresting questions" of national defence, nor did they think of their proposals primarily in terms of their effect on the Navy, or the nation. Responsibility and accountability to Parliament were their objects.[2]

This political approach to the problems of naval administration was not the only legacy of the early years of the century. The political views of key figures in the Admiralty were again to play a crucial part. The government of Derby and Disraeli had of course appointed a Board of their own political opinions—which were those of the great majority of mid-Victorian flag officers. There was, however, one man in an influential position who was a strong Liberal. Sir Robert Spencer Robinson was Controller of the Navy from 1861 to 1871. The change of name of his office in 1860 from Surveyor to Controller was expressive, for Robinson was the head of that part of the Admiralty, concerned with the design and construction of ships and the management of the dockyards, which corresponded closely to the old Navy Board. He inherited with the name a large measure of the independent power of the old Comptroller. In any age the job was bound to have been an important and powerful one, but in the 1860s it was of cardinal importance, for the Navy was at last entering the new industrial world. When Robinson became Controller the Navy possessed only two ironclads, the first in the world. When he left office there were no wooden sail of the line left in the battle fleet. Iron, steam and breech-loading guns had suddenly and completely upset the tranquil and orderly technical progress of previous years. Robinson was a man of commanding intellect, familiar with the new inventions and alive to their implications as few other admirals were. He was ambitious, unscrupulous and unpopular. Like Middleton eighty years before, he made no secret of his desire to have a seat at the Board, and with it a practical supremacy. As a subordinate of the First Sea Lord he had great influence; as a colleague, with the largest and most important part of naval administration at his command, he would be the real leader of the naval lords.[3]

H. C. E. Childers, who was appointed First Lord by Gladstone when he came to power in December 1868, saw in Robinson, his fellow-Liberal, a natural ally. Reactionary Tory sea lords might obstruct the wishes of Parliament and the Treasury, but with the Controller on his side, Childers could outflank the Board and capture the core of the administration. It is doubtful if any First Lord who entered office with no knowledge of the Navy and a doctrinaire determination to reduce it would ever have been popular with his naval colleagues, but Childers made no effort to win their support. His brusque and offensive manner, his unconcealed belief that all power over the Navy was vested in him alone, and his disinclination to take advice, did not endear him.[4]

Childers's reforms were embodied in an Order in Council in January 1869, less than a month after he had taken office. By this the Board was in effect, though not in name, abolished. Its members no longer met together except, on infrequent occasions, for purely formal purposes. Each Lord was now the executive head of his branch, for which he alone was answerable to the First Lord. All communication between Board members was in writing, and Childers took advice when, and from whom, he chose, inviting them singly to his room. Sir Spencer Robinson acquired his seat at the Board as "Third Lord and Controller", and his departments were moved from Somerset House (where they had been since 1786) to the houses in Spring Gardens from which the naval lords were ejected. The staff of the Admiralty was reduced in a year from 586 to 537, and the seamen of the Navy by five thousand.[5]

Childers's new system was in almost all practical respects disastrous. Co-ordination between Admiralty departments virtually ceased, and an already slender capacity to deal with the ever-increasing mass of technical business was crippled. Decisions of policy became the sole prerogative of the First Lord, and the naval lords were reduced, in name and in fact, to his "assistants". No decision was too technical for Childers to take himself, and in one bizarre and nearly fatal incident, he attempted to take personal command of the fleet during manoeuvres. The naval lords, overwhelmed by the quantity as well as the growing complexity of the work which remorselessly weighed upon them, entirely without naval staff,[6] humiliated and oppressed by Childers, ceased to have any effective control over naval policy. Robinson, who alone possessed the strength of character and intellect to stand up to Childers, proved a wayward ally and an ungovernable subordinate, and was out of office in little more than a year. The rest of the Board lacked political and professional standing, and were helpless under a ruthless political chief with support in Cabinet. The Board, which had met 249 times in 1866, had but thirty-three meetings in 1870, none lasting over half an hour.[7]

By abolishing the Board as a working instrument, Childers had set out to establish unbreakable chains of responsibility, all leading to himself. In this, at least, he ought to have succeeded. Whatever ill the changes wrought, there could be no more uncertainty over who was answerable for the Navy after Childers had taken charge. He alone took all major decisions. Among them was the decision to complete and send to sea H.M.S. *Captain*, the revolutionary new turret ship. This battleship was in effect the Liberals' answer to Tory naval architecture; designed, built and supported by Childers's political friends, she was intended to show the naval world the enlightened spirit of scientific progress at sea. She foundered on her maiden voyage with the loss of almost all on board. Whatever the technical questions raised by her loss, there could hardly have been a clearer case of a chain of responsibility leading directly to Childers. He was unquestionably answerable not only for his own decision to send the *Captain* to sea when some doubt existed as to her stability, but for the failures of his subordinates over whom he had so publicly and so completely taken authority. It might be supposed that he could hardly have avoided resignation. Instead, he wrote a minute which none of his colleagues saw until it was published in the newspapers "by Command of their Lordships", in which, in the name of the whole Board, he flatly exonerated himself and laid the whole blame on subordinates who could not defend themselves.[8]

It is scarcely necessary to comment on this remarkable episode, except to say that Childers, who had slept little for years and whose son had gone down with the *Captain*, was probably on the verge of a nervous breakdown. Well or ill, it was eminently characteristic of his methods. Almost as soon as the minute was published the Admiralty was embroiled in a fierce political row, in the course of which Sir Spencer Robinson was personally dismissed by Gladstone, and Sir Edward Reed, the Chief Naval Architect, resigned—these being the two principally blamed by Childers for the loss of a ship which they had neither designed nor approved. On 13th March 1871 Childers followed them, broken in health and spirits and unlamented by all who had worked with him.[9]

Even at this stage, it seems very unlikely if anyone outside the Admiralty (or many within it) understood the ways in which Childers had really failed. The embarrassment he had brought on the governments, even the loss of 481 lives, were of little importance to the future of the Navy beside the virtual abolition of any machinery for reviewing and settling policy. The Navy was entering an era of more rapid and decisive technical change than ever before in its history, and there was no hand on the tiller.

G. J. Goschen, who inherited the now disorganized and demoralised Admiralty, was a wise and tolerant administrator, well chosen to patch the wounds Childers had opened, but he had too much to do trying to make the system work at all to make further radical changes. He did, however, introduce two measures designed to mitigate the worst of Childers's excesses; he removed the Controller from the Board, and he instituted weekly Board meetings, supplemented by "Daily Meetings" to improve co-ordination and mutual information. Lastly, he re-appointed as First Naval Lord Sir Alexander Milne, a Tory who had formerly served in Disraeli's time. The change was a symbolical one, but none the less important, for Milne was the first senior naval lord to be appointed by a ministry of the opposite party, and so the first to be explicitly recognized as a professional rather than a party appointment. By his alterations in procedure, and still more by his tolerant and humane spirit, Goschen made Childers's system workable. In the opinion of a Secretary of the Admiralty writing in the 1920s he was the real author of the modern Admiralty. Nevertheless, he wrought no fundamental changes. He was content to ameliorate the evils of a system which was in two respects radically unsatisfactory, and seen by acute contemporaries to be so. It did not provide any central directing authority, any "brain", and it lacked the capacity to understand and make use of the new technologies. The Navy entered an age of unprecedented material change largely unfitted to cope with it.[10]

Naval affairs, moreover, remained as uninteresting for politicians as ever. Only as a source of expense did the Service attract the least attention. The First Lords of the 1870s, Goschen, G. W. Hunt and W. H. Smith, were men of their times; they conscientiously presented the case for the Navy, but they never seriously expected to get what they asked for. For the most part they accepted that real reform or expansion of the Navy was a quixotic idea, and as practical men they did not tilt at windmills. Ward Hunt was described by Disraeli to Queen Victoria as having "the sagacity of an elephant as well as its form". His form was so substantial that a semi-circular piece had to be cut from the end of the Board Room table to accommodate it, but at the Cabinet table, he carried little weight. "There never was a more just nor more inopportune demand preferred", a subordinate remarked sadly of Hunt's vain efforts to get more money for the Navy. When he died in 1877 the Board of Admiralty followed him sorrowing to the grave, but declined to carry the coffin. His successor, W. H. Smith, was an equally able and popular administrator, and of equally slender standing in Cabinet. W. S. Gilbert has unkindly immortalised him as Sir Joseph Porter K. C. B., who stuck close to his desk and never went to sea, and so became the ruler of the Queen's Navy. Nothing, in fact, was more typical of a First Lord than to have seen no ship but a partnership before taking office, and in this, as in his attitudes, Smith fitted the mould of the age. Naval affairs deserved and received devoted administration, but they stood on the periphery of public life, lacking the popular appeal of theology or drains.[11]

Many naval officers accepted the Navy's essentially subordinate rôle without question. They never behaved as though they believed that, under God, the wealth, safety and strength of the kingdom chiefly depended on them, or even that the Navy might one day be at war. There were, however, far-sighted officers who saw the weaknesses of the Admiralty and tried to overcome them. Milne was one of them, and another was Sir Geoffrey Phipps Hornby. Hornby attempted to form a compact with two contemporaries who were his only rivals for the First Sea Lordship, each undertaking to refuse office unless they were granted at least the skeleton of a naval staff. Hornby himself did refuse, but in 1879 Sir Astley Cooper Key accepted. A worse choice to meet the Navy's pressing need for breadth of understanding and strength of character could not easily have been found. Key was a born administrator, if by that is meant someone who loves work and hates decisions. An essentially weak man, he crowded his desk, his day and his mind with comforting trivia, and carefully excluded anything so unsettling as policy. Worse, when Gladstone returned to power in May 1880 he appointed as First Lord Lord Northbrook, an expert on India, finance and the colonies, whose advice on these matters was more sought after by his Cabinet colleagues than his work in a department which neither he nor they valued highly. So long as the Estimates were kept down, Northbrook was content to leave the running of the Navy to those, like Key, who enjoyed it.[12]

The combination of Northbrook and Key could not have been worse for the Navy. For a decade the crucial questions which had to be answered almost daily in that age of bewildering change, especially those of ship design and gunnery, went largely by default, or were settled by subordinates. Gunnery questions, indeed, were not even under naval control. The War Office, inheriting the duties of the Ordnance Board, supplied the Navy's guns and ammunition. It was quite capable of issuing gunnery fittings which the Admiralty had never approved, or even seen, and it refused to reveal, if it knew itself, what, if any, reserves of shell were held in readiness for war. Within the Admiralty co-ordination was not much better. The ever-growing size of the Office made it impossible for the Secretary's Office to be, as it once had been, the channel of all communications and the repository of all knowledge. In particular the Controller's departments, which were largely responsible for the new technology, had grown to dominate the Admiralty intellectually as well as in point of numbers. In the 1880s the Controller had under him Directors of Naval Construction, of Naval Ordnance, of Dockyards and of Stores, the Inspector of Dockyard Expense Accounts, and the Engineer-in-Chief, each of whom in their turn controlled large departments. Such naval staff as existed was almost all in the Controller's departments.[13]

All this made it still more difficult for weak and uninterested Boards, submerged in trivia, to provide either the co-ordination or the direction the Navy so badly needed. Ships were designed and built in whose conception the Board had had only a nominal rôle. Insofar as the ill-assorted fleets of the 1870s and early 1880s reflected any policy, it came not from the Board but from the Director of Naval Construction, drawn into the vacuum caused by its abdication of power.[14]

Much of this was to change with remarkable swiftness in the late 1880s. The mid-Victorian public had a sentimental affection for the Navy, but it neither knew nor thought much about it. In the 1880s a new spirit was abroad. Social Darwinism and the victory of Prussian discipline and preparedness, among other factors, taught people to value naval strength and worry about naval unpreparedness. The time was near at hand when the public would accept, and even demand, a Navy superior to all others. Between the day in September 1884 when the first of W. T. Stead's articles on "The Truth about the Navy" was published in the *Pall Mall Gazette*, and the passing of the Naval Defence Act in 1889, which provided for a Navy built to a two-power standard, less than five years elapsed, but in that time a fundamental change in public opinion came to fruition. From vying with one another for economy, the parties changed to encouraging or accommodating popular pressure for a larger Navy. The most dramatic symbol of the reversal of public attitudes was the fall of Gladstone in 1894, his long public career ended, in part because he would not bow to the new cry for naval expenditure.[15]

The Admiralty had now to cope with a rapid expansion of the Navy, and a consequent increase in its own staff. In organization, however, it remained the Admiralty which Goschen had patched up out of the ruins of Childers's reforms. There was still no effective mechanism for deciding policy and no adequate naval staff to handle material questions. To some extent the great abilities of such men as Lord George Hamilton, First Lord from 1886 to 1892, Sir Frederick Richards, First Sea Lord from 1893 to 1899 (one of the rare sailors of modern times able to stand up to the Cabinet), and George Goschen, who returned as First Lord for the last five years of the century, concealed the weakness of the system, and there were some attempts to improve it. The Naval Intelligence Division was founded in 1886 with the specific intention that it should form the nucleus of a naval staff, and its work in that rôle was of great value, but it remained a malnourished shoot among the spreading branches of the Admiralty. Even if there had existed a developed naval staff it is doubtful if it could have achieved much in the absence of intelligent political support. Politicians appreciated the need to meet public demand for a great navy, but they thought little, and to little purpose, about war. They expected the Admiralty to provide day-to-day administration, and hardly understood that anything more might be asked of it, or indeed of them. "At the close of the nineteenth century the system of central government could virtually ignore the demands of war, and was still not attuned in many respects to the implications of an industrial society". At the same time the Navy was not only expanding but changing very fast. Every year new types of ships and weapons were introduced, every year new possibilities in warfare opened up. Naval men and Admiralty clerks were fully occupied in keeping abreast of developments. There was no time for reflection on the implications of these novelties, no leisure to formulate policy. The pressure of the times and the weakness of the system obscured all but present concerns.[16]

Nevertheless, the Admiralty was compelled by the nature of its responsibilities to adapt to the new material world. The War Office not only had no machinery to direct policy but was so inefficient that in 1886 it completely mislaid a regiment, in England, in peacetime. It was still possible for the army to behave as if nothing had changed since 1815; for the Navy, the problem was to remember that some things had not, in particular the principles of naval strategy. The new technology led the Admiralty into becoming a pioneer of scientific research. Earlier in the century it had sponsored hydrography and exploration, now it expended large sums on hydrodynamics and metallurgy. For a government department of the day this was extraordinary, if not unique.[17]

The increasing size of the Navy and its civil establishments obliged them to develop more efficient methods of management and accounting. Even in 1882, before the great expansion began, the dockyards employed nearly 20,000 men, and Portsmouth alone had 6,256. Though they had lost their seventeenth- and eighteenth-century pre-eminence, they were still some of the largest and most complex industrial organizations in the country, and (notwithstanding the opinion of the time) among the most efficient.[18]

The pressure of change, both natural and artificial, had on the one hand almost destroyed the Admiralty's original rôle as a body for the co-ordination and direction of high policy, and on the other enormously amplified the administrative duties of the old Navy Board. As an administrative body, the Admiralty of the last years of the century was still surprisingly efficient in spite of the long years of peace, but it was undoubtedly an easy-going and idiosyncratic organization, if not, as *The Times* described it, "a very ancient and peculiar corporation". The higher clerks were supposed to work from 10.30 a.m. until 6 p.m., with every other Saturday off, but the hours were not adhered to. When Charles Walker, the first university graduate ever to enter the Secretary's department, arrived at ten o'clock on his first morning in 1895, he was met by an astonished old messenger with the words, "Lord bless you, Sir, there won't none of them be here yet; go away and come back at a quarter to eleven." The fact that university men like Walker and Oswyn Murray, who came down from Oxford two years later with a triple First and the Vinerian Scholarship, were now called for in an office once concerned largely with copying, was a sign of the great responsibilities the Admiralty was undertaking, but in the 1890s they had not yet made any great revolution in office procedure. Though the Registry clerks were supposed to have opened and marked all the several hundred letters and papers which came in daily by ten o'clock, the papers moved more slowly in their progress round the Office. It was thought unusual for a docket to be dealt with in so little time as two months. Telegrams were uncommon, and a cypher telegram so rare as to cause quite a stir in the Military Branch where it was decoded. Typewriters were unknown, and all copying was by letter press. There was only a single telephone in the Admiralty, on a special table outside the First Lord's room, and only the most senior officials were permitted to touch it—a dangerous privilege, as it gave off vivid sparks when used. There were some unofficial channels of communication faster than these: one old messenger made a good income for years out of a private intelligence system whereby he could give officers news of promotions and appointments well in advance of official notification. The garden remained, with its wicket gate through which old Lord Barham, by special permission when ill, had taken short cuts across St James's Park to his home in Birdcage Walk ninety years before. Tennis was played on the lawn beneath the Board Room windows at least as late as 1899.[19]

The Admiralty was remarkably conscious, and proud, of its traditions. Senior clerks read and quoted Pepys, showing a strong awareness of the history of the Navy and the Office. When the Public Record Office declared a large amount of old Navy Board records to be not worth preserving, the Admiralty indignantly refused to allow them to be destroyed, and went to some trouble and expense to preserve them themselves—a decision for which historians will ever bless them.[20]

The growth of the Admiralty finally made it impossible to cram everyone into the Old Building and the houses in Spring Gardens, and in 1892 a new building, "in the style of a Midland town hall", was begun at right angles to the old, facing across Horse Guards Parade. Early in the new century, the houses in Spring Gardens were demolished to connect the Mall with Trafalgar Square, and finally the Admiralty Arch was completed in 1911, providing a home for the Admiralty Library in its crown.[21]

By 1896 nearly one fifth of all government expenditure went on the Navy. A quarter of a million people worked for or in the Service, or in industries which directly depended on it, which was 2¼ per cent of the total workforce of the country. The Admiralty built and maintained an enormous fleet, it specified, designed and often manufactured every variety of stores from chamber-pots to torpedoes. It fed, clothed and supervised its officers and men from boyhood to the grave, and to a considerable extent their wives and children with them. In an age when the state hardly impinged on the affairs of most of its citizens, and was only beginning to interfere in the economic life of the nation, the Admiralty represented a complete society in miniature; an industrial society, and a welfare state half a century before the state itself assumed that rôle. The Navy was remarkably self-contained. It depended on no other department of government for any essential supply, except of course money (and, until 1907, in part for guns). It believed, with some reason, that there was very little it could not do, and very little it should not attempt. Though there was sometimes friction between clerks and naval officers at the Admiralty, the civilians had a real affection for the Navy, and a sense of belonging to a wider naval family. The Director of Victualling, for example, insisted on inspecting personally every type of stores he ordered for the fleet, so that in his room "samples of sailor's caps, boots, serge, raisins, sugar, chocolate, flannel strewed the table that stood under a mysterious glass case, in which was a single ship's biscuit, centuries old".[22]

The Admiralty of the 1890s was a remarkable, and in many respects unique institution, but it was not in any real sense the true heir of the Admiralty of the Napoleonic Wars. It was really the inheritor of the functions of the Navy Board. It undoubtedly discharged them better than the Navy Board had done, indeed as an administrative body the late nineteenth-century Admiralty was excellent by the standards of its day, but it had lost its original functions as a directing and co-ordinating body for naval policy. Two major reforms and several minor ones had completely effaced the old system and its ways. The Navy entered the new century with the engines running sweetly, and no-one at the helm. Yet so little was that appreciated that in 1903 Viscount Esher was appointed chairman of a committee to reconstruct the delinquent War Office, humiliated by the disasters of the South African War, in the image and likeness of the Admiralty:

> "We are directed by the terms of our Reference to take the Admiralty system of higher administration as the basis of our action, and we are

convinced that, while there may be imperfections in the working of that system, it is absolutely sound in principle. It has been handed down without material change from the period of the great naval wars. It may be said to have been founded on the proved requirements of war, and although it has not in recent times been put to the supreme test, it has smoothly and successfully met new demands as they have arisen, including an enormous increase of personnel and material. It conforms closely to the arrangements under which the largest private industries are conducted. Finally, it has retained the confidence of the Navy and of the Nation."

The reader will be able to judge how far this view was from the truth.[23]

NOTES

1 Dewar, *Aspects of Organisation*, 4.

2 Wright, *Treasury Control*, 269. Johnson, *Defence by Committee*, 13.

3 Rodger, MM LXI, 12-14. Colomb, *Memoirs of Key*, 379.

4 Hamilton, *Naval Administration*, 24. Colomb, 382. Rodger, MM LXI, 338-339. Murray, VII, 473.

5 Murray, I, 30. Smith, MM IX, 280, Wright, 186-187. Rodger, MM LXI, 335.

6 In 1870 there were sixteen naval officers in the Admiralty Office, ten of them in the Hydrographer's Department, the rest mostly in the Controller's.

7 Murray, VII, 471-473. Rodger, MM LXI, 336, 339. Hamilton, *Naval Administration*, 25.

8 Rodger, MM LXI, 339.

9 Briggs, 190. Rodger, MM LXI, 340.

10 Briggs, 196. Murray, VII, 475. Hamilton, *Naval Administration*, 158. Rodger, MM LXI, 340-343.

11 *Ante* p. 104. Rodger, MM LXII, 33, 39. Chilston, *W.H. Smith*, 93n.1, 104. Briggs, 200-201.

12 Rodger, MM LXII, 34-35, 38, 121. Briggs, 210-211.

13 Hamilton, *Naval Administration*, 60, 67-68, 80. Colomb, 355. In 1880 there were twenty-three naval officers in the Admiralty; twelve in the Hydrographer's department, almost all the rest in the Controller's.

14 Rodger, MM LXII, 41-48.

15 Rodger, MM LXII, 37, 126; LXIII, 33.

16 Colomb, 327. Mackay, *Fisher,* 376, 209-210. Marder, *Anatomy of British Sea Power* [*ABSP*], 242-244. Rodger, MM LXII, 123-126. Ehrman, *Cabinet Government & War*, vii. Schurman, *Education of a Navy*, 103. Cowpe, "Royal Navy & Torpedo", 36.

17 Johnson, 37. Fay, *War Office at War,* 15. Lyon, "Admiralty & Industry", 44-47.

18 Ashworth, EcHR 2° XXII, 493-497.

19 Hankey, *Supreme Command* I, 24. *Times* leader of 15th March 1905. Walker, *Thirty-Seven Years*, 9-10, 13, 15. Murray, *Making of a Civil Servant*, 35, 46, 54. ADM 1/9196. Corbett, *Spencer MSS* I, 45.

20 Murray, *Civil Servant,* 36. ADM 1/9463.

21 McLachlan, *Room 39*, 1. Smith, MM IX, 281-282.

22 Ashworth, 491-492. Murray I, 13. Murray, *Civil Servant*, 64-68. Mackay, *Fisher*, 191-192. For the probable age of the biscuit, see Hamilton, *Naval Administration*, 116.

23 Murray, VII, 478.

CHAPTER EIGHT

BOARDS OF ADMIRALTY 1904-1918

First Lords:

12th November 1900	William Palmer, Earl of Selborne
27th March 1905	Frederick Campbell, Earl Cawdor
22nd December 1905	Edward Marjoribanks, Lord Tweedmouth
16th April 1908	Reginald McKenna
24th October 1911	Winston Churchill
27th May 1915	Arthur Balfour
11th December 1916	Sir Edward Carson
20th July 1917	Sir Eric Geddes

First Sea Lords:

14th August 1899	Lord Walter Kerr
20th October 1904	Sir John Fisher
25th January 1910	Sir Arthur Wilson
5th December 1911	Sir Francis Bridgeman
9th December 1912	Prince Louis of Battenberg
30th October 1914	John, Lord Fisher
27th May 1915	Sir Henry Jackson
4th December 1916	Sir John Jellicoe
10th January 1918	Sir Rosslyn Wemyss

Permanent Secretaries:

2nd April 1884	Sir Evan Macgregor
9th May 1907	Sir Inigo Thomas
2nd October 1911	Sir William Graham Greene
7th August 1917	Sir Oswyn Murray

CHAPTER EIGHT

Inscrutable Providence

"In the eyes of the Royal Navy the Admiralty may be said to represent practically all the departments of state rolled into one. Indeed, it does more than represent all the departments of state. It discharges, in addition, most of the functions of an inscrutable Providence."[1]

Sir Oswyn Murray, Secretary of the Admiralty, 1917-1936

THE Navy and the Admiralty at the turn of the century were weakest in strategical and directive, and strongest in technical and administrative powers. Nevertheless, they were far from being technically perfect. Half a century had passed since the last of Nelson's captains had left the Service, and even the dimmest memories of major war at sea had faded. Breadth of mind and breadth of knowledge were uncommon in senior officers, and intellectual formation was largely lacking. The Navy was a conservative body, its officers drawn from a narrow social background, and denied the education of other men of their class. Inevitably, it was in many respects in need of re-organization, and still more in need of shaking up. War was for most officers a very distant and unlikely prospect, and preparation for it consequently unexciting and inessential. From their memoirs one might be pardoned for supposing that their sole professional pride was seamanship, and their sole private recreation snipe-shooting. This was not in fact true of the best officers, who were earnest students of warfare, but their studies were highly theoretical, if not altogether unreal. Like theologians, they approached a subject with which they had of necessity an imperfect acquaintance, and like theologians, they sometimes forgot the limitations of their knowledge. This placid world was urgently in need of change, and it was to have it.

On 20th October 1904, the eve of the ninety-ninth anniversary of the Battle of Trafalgar, Sir John Fisher arrived at the Admiralty as First Sea Lord. He was probably the most remarkable man ever to have sat at the Board of Admiralty, which had seldom wanted for ability and character. Men hated or worshipped Fisher, but none was neutral, and half a century after his death, his name has not ceased to arouse strong feeling. For more than ten years Fisher dominated the Navy absolutely. He was a man of extraordinary, almost demonic, energy and unbridled enthusiasm. He often began work as early as four o'clock, and was never at his desk later than six. Only a personal order from the King kept him from it on Sundays. His enormous appetite for work, his hypnotic personality, so ruthless, yet so persuasive, formed a combination of qualities unequalled before or since, and his achievements at the Admiralty decisively altered naval, and perhaps world history.[2] The training of naval officers was radically revised to abolish the official and social distinctions between executive and engineer officers, and to improve the technical education of the former. The pay and conditions of the lower deck, to which Fisher always devoted great concern, were greatly improved. A revolutionary new battleship, H.M.S. *Dreadnought,* was built in a year and a day, rendering all other battleships obsolete at once. Scores of old warships were scrapped and their crews turned over to more productive tasks. Control of naval guns was at last won from the War Office, and the standards of naval gunnery improved out of all recognition.[3]

Under firm supervision, Fisher was almost entirely a force for good. Hardly anybody, however, was able to exercise firm supervision over such a man. With unchallenged mastery he could have been diplomatic and conciliatory, had it been in his character. He cared nothing for conventions and precedents, except to break them. Indeed, he had no taste for consensus: "I am here kicking everybody's shins just to let them know that I am here", he wrote; it was his usual approach. His friends urged him to "play upon the delicate instrument of public opinion with your fingers and not with your feet", but in vain. His methods were often devious and unscrupulous; he corresponded secretly with junior officers about their seniors, and the press about Admiralty policy. Though not unwilling to take advice, from those who had the courage to proffer it, he brooked no opposition. He could break the careers of those who disagreed with him with a vindictiveness which the politicians of two centuries before had not shown. His feud with Lord Charles Beresford, an officer who in talents if not in character resembled him, and whose ideas were in some ways in advance of his, split the Navy and ruined the careers of many officers the country could ill afford to lose.[4]

Fisher has often been hailed as the great moderniser of the Navy, as the man who hauled it kicking and screaming into the twentieth century. This is true, but it would be equally accurate to regard him as the last of the Victorians. His faults were those of his predecessors, magnified. He was an enthusiastic rather than a deep thinker, whose mind dealt naturally in slogans and superficialities. His brilliance as an administrator was not matched by strategic intuition. Like many of the Liberal-leaning reformers of the previous century, he more than half believed that economy and reform were natural associates, and he too hankered after some small and cheap warship to overturn the ancient dominance of the battleship. He was an uncritical enthusiast for new developments and new weapons, although his technical knowledge was relatively limited. This has gained him the reputation of a prophet, but in truth many of his prophecies were very wrong, and hardly any were very specific. His thinking on submarines, of which he had some claim to be godfather, was a "mixture of vision and confusion". He held that marine engines would soon be so reliable that no engineers would be needed. He was a complete autocrat and centraliser, refusing to delegate any function of importance. He gathered brilliant men about him, and gave them nothing to do. In power he forgot his former support for a naval staff as soon as he realised that it might threaten his authority — especially as it was the principal proposal of his arch-rival Beresford.[5]

Like so many reformers, Fisher was a social conservative, who hated typewriters and shorthand. For all his undoubted brilliance and his extraordinary achievements, he lacked the intellect to break free from his inherited prejudices, and his force of character indelibly stamped the Service with an exaggerated version of the very faults which both had inherited. After Fisher, the Navy was more obsessed with *matériel* and more careless of strategy and policy; lacking a staff, it was grossly ill-equipped to manage a modern war, and was quite unaware of the fact. It can fairly be said that Fisher, great as his achievements were, was in many respects a disastrous influence on the Navy, and he cannot escape blame for the shortcomings and failures revealed by the war.[6]

In the early years of the century informed public opinion was becoming concerned about the Cabinet's central direction of the fighting services, or the lack of it. As early as 1895 an "august but ineffective body", the Cabinet Defence Committee, had been appointed, but it had no secretariat, no defined powers or duties, and no support by the Cabinet. The disasters of the Boer War upset public complacency, and the first reaction was to seek a scapegoat in the War Office, popularly contrasted with that model of efficiency, the Admiralty. Viscount Esher's South Africa Committee was followed by another Committee under his chairmanship specifically charged with remaking the War Office in the image and likeness of the Admiralty. Fisher was a member, intended to guide the Esher Committee's deliberations as Middleton had guided the Commissioners on Fees in Public Offices – though it is unlikely that he had been expected to turn up at the first meeting with the final report already written in his pocket, as he did. The Navy and the Admiralty were at the height of their popularity; administrative reformers tried to establish an Army Council in imitation of the Admiralty Board, and those who strove for a machinery for the central direction of war were biased in favour of the naval point of view. The Cabinet Defence Committee of 1902-1904, and even more the Committee of Imperial Defence which succeeded it, were in practice the instruments by which the Cabinet forced a recalcitrant War Office to accept the Admiralty's view of the army's rôle. The Committee of Imperial Defence's proponents thought of it as in some sense a nascent general staff for the Empire, and the Navy supported it because that implied both the Navy's primacy and its traditional rôle on the broad oceans of the world.[7]

All this changed with remarkable speed, because of a new strategic position. Fisher, ironically, was one of the first to draw attention to it by redistributing the fleets to meet the growing German threat. This threat, and the consequent entente with France, implied an enemy which the army rather than the Navy was best placed to resist. The situation was pregnant with difficulty for the Navy, but the War Office seized the opportunity eagerly. The General Staff began to plan for an expeditionary force to the Continent, and opened staff talks with the French. The Admiralty was forced onto the defensive. Fisher's answer was to propound plans for a seaborne landing in the Baltic. All the worst features of his thinking were combined in this proposal. He refused to disclose the nature of the plans, and of course there was no staff to work them out. They were made without military advice, and there is no doubt that they were on both naval and military grounds wholly impracticable. Fisher proposed to commit to landings in the Baltic the very troops the War Office intended to send to France. There was no agreed basis of strategy. The Cabinet members of the Committee of Imperial Defence found to their alarm that their service departments were preparing to go to war in completely unrelated and incompatible fashions, and not necessarily against the same enemy.[8]

Under pressure from the Cabinet to produce a war plan, and from Beresford and his friends to produce a staff, Fisher in 1906 appointed a small committee under Captain G. A. Ballard to draw up war plans. Ballard was an extremely clever and extremely taciturn man, who worked fast, and almost alone. The finished plan was produced in conditions of great secrecy, in only four copies, which were divulged to nobody outside the Admiralty. They were shown to nobody, but they were only for show. Ballard's plans, though as clever as their author, rested on no agreed basis of strategy, and in no way matched the complexity of modern war. The Ballard Committee was intended by Fisher simply as a sop to the unease of the public.[9]

Fisher was succeeded by his friend and disciple Sir A. K. Wilson, a sea commander of some ability but an administrator combining the worst of Fisher's faults with few of his virtues. He was obstinate, tactless, obsessively secretive, and quite unable to delegate. His powers of intellect were poor, and of self-expression non-existent. He held it as an article of faith that planning for war was neither practical nor desirable, though when pressed he insisted that there was a plan—in his head.[10]

In 1911 the Agadir Crisis brought Britain within measurable distance of war with Germany, and the Cabinet decided that it was no longer possible to leave the Admiralty and War Office to go their separate ways, unconnected with each other and unsubordinated to the Cabinet. With war apparently imminent, the First Sea Lord and the Director of Military Operations were urgently summoned to explain their plans to the Committee of Imperial Defence. At this critical juncture, Admiral Wilson and most of the Board were away shooting, but they were eventually found, and on 23rd August 1911 the meeting took place. General Sir Henry Wilson was a fluent and confident speaker, backed by a large staff, with a coherent and comprehensive war plan. Sir Arthur Wilson was a sorry contrast, his delivery rambling and almost unintelligible, his vaunted secret plan revealed as a few silly platitudes, devoid of serious thought. There was no real contest between naval and military strategy: the military strategy was the only credible one on offer.[11]

The effect on the Cabinet was immediate. Viscount Haldane, the Secretary for War, threatened to resign unless the Admiralty were forced to adopt a naval staff and plan for war, and Asquith appointed to the Admiralty the young and energetic Home Secretary, Winston Churchill. Churchill was not at first a naval expert, but he set about becoming one with zeal. In his first eighteen months in office he spent 182 days at sea. In temperament and methods he fell somewhere between Sandwich and Childers: like Sandwich, he was a politician of noble birth, who made it his pride to master the technicalities of the naval world; like Childers, he "claimed and exercised an unlimited power of suggestion" in matters which he understood, half-understood, or did not understand at all.[12]

Churchill took early steps to dismiss Wilson, appointing in his place Sir Francis Bridgeman, a colourless man, with judgement, but no force of character. Churchill's most urgent task was to institute a naval staff. There had existed since 1909 a powerless advisory body called the Naval War Council, presided over by the First Sea Lord—or rather, not, for Fisher and Wilson intended it only as a cosmetic measure, and took good care that it should not often meet. This Churchill took as the nucleus of the Naval War Staff created in 1912. It had three Divisions (Operations, Mobilization and Intelligence) reporting to the Chief of War Staff, who was an officer of comparable seniority to the First Sea Lord, but not a member of the Board.[13]

Both in theory and in practice the new arrangement was unsatisfactory. The staff was purely advisory, and no-one was obliged to listen to it. It was concerned almost entirely with planning and not execution, so the weakness of the Admiralty in controlling a complex modern war was scarcely ameliorated. The Chief of War Staff stood in an ambiguous relation to the First Sea Lord, neither a colleague nor a subordinate. Much of the "staff" consisted of the Naval Intelligence Division renamed – "the old dog had merely been provided with a War Staff collar". The quality of the staff themselves, lacking any proper training, and brought up in an exclusively technical school, was hardly equal to the task, and there was in any case no clear idea what was to be done. Most of the staff officers had been selected as too old, sick or incompetent to be sent to sea, and the few men of ability found themselves largely idle. Even if the best men had been concentrated in the Staff, it is doubtful if they could have made it work properly. "The brains and talents of the Navy had been mortgaged to Gunnery and the Fleets at sea, and, deflected for years into technical channels, they still continued to flow in the same direction".[14]

Churchill leant heavily on Fisher as an unofficial First Sea Lord. They shared a boyish enthusiasm for technical developments and a similar concern for the lower deck, and their greatest achievements were in these areas. The discipline, pay and promotion prospects of the seamen were greatly improved by Churchill. Oil fuel was introduced, and a controlling share in the Anglo-Persian Oil Company purchased to provide it. The Admiralty enthusiastically promoted the development of aeroplanes. These were advances of great importance, and Churchill and Fisher can deservedly take credit for them. They did not, however, touch on the Admiralty's crucial weakness – its inability to direct the conduct of a modern war, or to take hold of issues of policy – and the Naval War Staff had not greatly changed the position. Churchill and Fisher themselves, and Prince Louis of Battenberg who was First Sea Lord from 1912 to 1914, were all men of great, even extraordinary abilities, but they none of them wholly escaped the conventional outlook of their times. The conventional outlook was about to be cruelly tested.[15]

The nation, and the Navy, entered in the summer of 1914 on a war for which they were in organization and outlook wholly unprepared. Neither the Cabinet nor the Admiralty possessed any effective means of formulating naval policy, and the Admiralty was ill-equipped to execute it. The wireless aerials rigged on masts on the roof might impress the uninitiated, but they scarcely betokened a directing intelligence within. Elsewhere in Whitehall, the Committee of Imperial

Defence was succeeded first by the War Council, and then in June 1915 by the Dardanelles Committee, and in November 1915 by a new War Committee, without markedly improving the higher direction of the war. At the Admiralty, too, an "inner Cabinet", the War Group, assumed direction, consisting of Churchill the First Lord, Fisher the First Sea Lord (succeeding Battenberg who was compelled to resign late in 1914), the Chief of War Staff, the Secretary, the First Lord's Naval Secretary, and Sir A. K. Wilson, who held no official post. The junior sea lords were ignored, and, as Churchill put it, "fell naturally and automatically to some extent into the position of the old Navy Office". This they protested about, but in vain, for Churchill had all precedent on his side, and knew it.[16]

The real cause of their dissatisfaction, however, was less the constitutional form than the practical manner of Churchill's management. He had always interfered with the Navy, often to the fury of admirals, and he did not cease at the outbreak of war. His admiration for Fisher, undimmed in 1914, began to fade rapidly with closer acquaintance. By 1914 Fisher had lost none of his reputation or his popularity with the public, but his powers were declining, and the demands of war showed to least advantage a man who had no use for a staff, whose strategic sense was poor, and whose tolerance for colleagues was fading fast. Churchill and Fisher fought each other as energetically as they fought the Germans, each claiming that the other acted without consulting him, while the junior sea lords, like a Greek chorus from the side, vainly proclaimed that it was they "who should be the real War Staff of the Navy". Meanwhile the Chief of War Staff, Sir Doveton Sturdee, kept all papers to himself, and the junior sea lords were left to learn of such events as the Antwerp and Dardanelles expeditions from rumour, or from the newspapers. Fisher's self-restraint, never his most prominent virtue, had entirely gone, and his colleagues became alarmed for his sanity. In this sorry condition, with the Cabinet unable to control the war, and the Admiralty unable to control itself, the nation found itself involved in the Dardanelles campaign.[17]

After a year of war on a scale never hitherto imagined, and in circumstances unseen and unprovided for, the Admiralty's hold over operations was weak and fumbling. More than a century before, in the midst of another desperate struggle, Barham had understood and embodied the distinction between administrative and operational control, and had achieved both. The development of wireless, in a war fought largely in home waters, transformed the Admiralty's position. Intelligently used, it offered the chance to strengthen the hand of the flag officer at sea with information faster and more complete than had ever been possible. It also played into the hands of anyone who was by nature a remote controller. Under Sturdee, pompous and inflexible, and his abler successor Sir Henry Oliver, all administration was concentrated in the War Staff, and actual staff work was scarcely undertaken. Planning was largely abandoned under the pressure of war, but control of operations was scarcely improved thereby. The Operations Division lacked any creative thought, and in practice had little to do with operations. "Neither the Chief of the War Staff nor the Director of Operations Division seemed to have any particular idea of what the War Staff was supposed to be doing, or how they should make use of it". Those unwise enough to offer unpalatable advice to their seniors ran some risk of disciplinary action. The staff officers were the weaker members of a generation whose training had been exclusively concerned with *matériel* and administration, and whose general education was gravely deficient. The wireless channels were crowded with such matters as the issue of lime juice and the private affairs of Ordinary Seamen, and in the Admiralty "round and round go the dockets solemn slow stately and sure, and meanwhile the ships are being sent rapidly to the bottom." The disaster of Coronel was largely attributable to poor staff work, and it was remarkably fortunate that the Heligoland Bight action did not turn out the same way, as the Admiralty contrived to have three squadrons in the same area each unaware of the others' presence, and then confused latitude and longitude in plotting them. As late as 1916, after two years of war, it was still sending forces to operate together without telling them that other British ships were at sea. Its incompetence at cyphering and decyphering caused confusion and delay, while many signals to the Admiralty went completely unanswered.[18]

Yet the Admiralty possessed at least one incalculable advantage, Sir Alfred Ewing, the Director of Naval Education, had recruited from his academic friends a small group, established in Room 40 of the Old

Building (from which they took their name) which by the outbreak of war was decyphering German naval wireless signals. An increasing stream of intelligence of the greatest importance came from Room 40. Yet the Operations Division neither valued nor trusted the cryptanalysts. They were forbidden to have any contact with the Naval Intelligence Division, and their material was sent "raw" to the War Room, without context or comment, to be made use of as the staff thought fit. The Director of the Operations Division, and many of his juniors, despised the cryptanalysts and their work. "Thank God," he exclaimed when the Germans changed their codes, "I shan't have any more of that damned stuff." The indifference or hostility of him and his staff to the work of Room 40 and the Naval Intelligence Division was largely responsible for the failure to win a decisive victory at Jutland.[19]

The fetish of centralisation was carried to extraordinary lengths. Sir Henry Oliver, Chief of War Staff after Sturdee, was untiring and efficient, but he had no interest in strategy, and could not delegate even his typing. With his own hand he drew up the sailing orders for thousands of ships, and plotted their movements on his chart. At the height of the war, Sir Henry Jackson, who succeeded Fisher as First Sea Lord, was concerning himself with the excessive wine-bills of junior officers on remote stations.

With centralisation went an obsession with secrecy. The impartial observer might consider that a secret is hardly worth preserving from the enemy at the expense of concealing it from one's friends, but the Admiralty disagreed. The naval attaché in Paris before the war had had to learn from his French contacts of naval staff conversations between their two countries. Within the Admiralty, Room 40 was forbidden to communicate with the German Section of N.I.D. and the Enemy Submarine Section, so that those who knew where the enemy was could not meet those who knew where British ships were. During the whole war, the Director of Naval Intelligence's private secretary never once entered Room 40. The staff of the Operations Division themselves were not always permitted to know the positions of important British ships at sea, so the master plot in the War Room, like Hamlet without the prince, showed the North Sea without the Grand Fleet. As strangers ranging from bishops to charwomen were often about the War Room, the plot was falsified to deceive them, and of course deceived others. The War Registry, which handled all signals and telegrams, was believed to be untrustworthy, so signals were made vague and misleading—with the natural result that the recipients were misled. British ships steamed into British minefields because the mining chart was too secret to be issued to them.[20]

The disaster of the Dardanelles campaign led to the dismissal of both Churchill and Fisher. In their place Asquith appointed Arthur Balfour and Sir Henry Jackson. For many they were a welcome change from the turbulent and quarrelsome pair they relieved. Balfour was a judicious and considerate First Lord, and had perhaps the finest mind in a government not composed of fools. Jackson was an able and sensible man, albeit prickly and withdrawn. Between them they supplied a balanced judgement which had often been lacking. Unhappily, it was at the expense of dynamism and imagination, and in 1915 the Admiralty could not afford to be complacent. Balfour's Board "will surely stand for a long time as one of the least effective Boards ever to rule the Navy — at any rate in time of war". In February 1915 the Germans declared a submarine blockade of the British Isles, and losses at once began to mount steeply. By the beginning of 1916 it was obvious that the situation was becoming critical, and those who had earlier welcomed Balfour's considerate and helpful manner now spoke of lethargy and indifference. When brought the news of ever more disastrous losses, Balfour complained wearily "it is very tiresome; these Germans are intolerable". His professional advisers were not much nearer the Nelson touch. By November 1916 Jackson and Oliver, the Chief of War Staff, were openly despairing of success against the submarine.[21]

It is no part of this study to explain how and why dissatisfaction with the conduct of the war finally brought down Asquith's government in December 1916, but the inaction of the Admiralty in the face of incipient disaster was not least of the causes, and not least of the things Lloyd George came determined to change. Sir Edward Carson, whom he appointed First Lord, is remembered for his remark that his only qualification for the job was that in naval matters he was all at sea, but in fact his acute mind and his willingness to learn did much to overcome that deficiency (so common among modern First Lords), and his tact and refusal to interfere in technical matters made him popular. At the same time his unwillingness to go beyond the proper and conventional procedures was to prove a weakness.[22]

Lloyd George's ideas for the Admiralty were not confined to a change of political head. At the same time Sir John Jellicoe was brought from the Grand Fleet to replace Jackson. Jellicoe's enormous prestige made the choice inevitable, but it must be doubted if it was wise. He was a man of many talents, but they were not those most in need. He was another obsessive centraliser, unable to delegate, devoted to administration and neglecting policy. "Sit in a chair," Carson advised him, "put your feet up, and think" — admirable advice, but Jellicoe was the last man to take it. "With all his talents, his mind was becoming less and less responsive to new ideas that conflicted with the cherished preconceptions that must have seemed to him like laws of nature." He did not welcome advice, unless it fitted his ideas, and he had no use for a staff. In the face of mounting losses from submarines, he had no answer but to hold his course. Councils, even the War Cabinet, were not for him the chance to decide policy, but a useless diversion from adminstration. "A tired and over-conscientious man in rather poor health who could not delegate business, constantly overworked himself and always saw the black side of things clearly", his pessimism so far affected the Cabinet that in March 1917 they were considering treating for peace on the best terms they could get. Under Churchill and Fisher the Admiralty had been turbulent and unreliable, but it had not wanted ideas. Under Jellicoe it set its face firmly against a real staff, and against the introduction of convoy. Carson was unhappy, but he could not bring himself to over-rule his professional advisers. Lloyd George had no such inhibitions.[23]

By the summer of 1917 officers and men at sea, and informed opinion on land, had lost confidence in the Admiralty, and the time was ripe, if not over-ripe, for change. There was not only dissatisfaction with Carson and his Board in person, but with the system. Even the *Daily Mail* had grasped the central point that the Admiralty Board "is a collection of heads of departments all so fully occupied with departmental work that they have no time for the hard thinking that is required in war."[24]

In July 1917 Carson was replaced by Sir Eric Geddes, and at the same time convoy was introduced and the naval staff re-organized. Jellicoe became both First Sea Lord and Chief of Staff, with a Deputy First Sea Lord to assist him. He now had, in theory at least, all the help he needed for his dual rôle of directing policy and operations, and the lines of command were clear and uncluttered. At long last Room 40 was united with the Naval Intelligence Division, and the Navy's extraordinary asset of intelligence made use of.[25]

Not the least important of Geddes's changes was in the Secretaryship. Sir William Graham Greene was "a dry old stick, a bachelor, devoted to the office, experienced, prudent and precise"; or, as Admiral Beatty more forthrightly called him, "one of those half dead men". He was undoubtedly able, but he was neither flexible nor imaginative, and his attitude to the new machinery of the Cabinet Office and to Hankey its Secretary was obstructive. His replacement by Sir Oswyn Murray "brought an entirely new vigour into the conduct of Admiralty business".[26]

Geddes himself was another source of renewed vigour. He was a railway engineer, a north-countryman who had worked his own way to the top. Ruthless, iconoclastic, blunt and self-confident, he was the last man to ingratiate himself with the Admiralty. As Controller for several months before becoming First Lord, he demanded and was granted the rank of Vice-Admiral (some while before he relinquished the rank of General which he had held in the War Office as Director of Transport) and wore his uniform. Knowing nothing of naval affairs before becoming Controller, "Goddis", as he was called behind his back, loathed the Admiralty and made no secret of his contempt. To this day, his name is remembered among naval officers with vituperation, and yet he must be counted one of the great First Lords of modern times. He came armed with complete Cabinet backing and a clear idea of what needed to be done. The Board, as he pointed out in a paper written in September, was as a Board too large effectively to control either policy or operations, "in fact in the present war the Board of Admiralty never has so functioned [*scil.* as a Board] and in my opinion cannot do so". It was central to Geddes's and the Cabinet's scheme that the First Sea Lord had to be freed of administrative worries to concentrate on the higher direction of the war at sea. To this end Geddes divided the Board into two committees; the Operations

Committee (First Sea Lord, Deputy First Sea Lord, Deputy and Assistant Chiefs of Naval Staff, plus the Fifth Sea Lord for the Naval Air Service) and the Maintenance Committee (Second, Third, and Fourth Sea Lords, Controller, Civil Lord, Financial Secretary, and Fifth Sea Lord if necessary). Both the two Committees, and the whole Board when it met to settle questions of principle, were given a regular procedure, with agenda and minutes. This division of responsibility was intended to free Jellicoe's hands, and at the same time he was specifically authorized to issue operational orders on his own authority.[27]

Geddes was in effect instituting a new version of the old distinction between Admiralty and Navy Office. The First Sea Lord and First Lord, supported by the Naval Staff, were to represent the Admiralty in its direction of policy and operational control, while the Maintenance Committee and the greater part of the Admiralty Office perpetuated the rôle of the Navy Board. As if to give point to the contrast, Geddes himself had been the first civilian Controller of the Navy since the seventeenth century, and he was succeeded by another, Sir Alan Anderson.[28]

Many of Geddes's intentions, however, were frustrated by the First Sea Lord and his immediate juniors. Jellicoe refused to delegate to the staff, treating the Deputy First Sea Lord, the Deputy and Assistant Chiefs of Naval Staff as junior officers not to be trusted with serious decisions. Every signal and paper, however trivial, had to be seen by Jellicoe, and the staff for their part did not think ahead but immersed themselves in routine. A Plans Division of the Staff, established against Jellicoe's bitter opposition (in a tiny attic without even a chart table), was largely ignored. "Congestion at the top and inertia at the bottom prevented investigation of alternative courses of action".[29]

By the end of 1917 Lloyd George and Geddes had become convinced that any reform which left Jellicoe as First Sea Lord would fail in its real purpose. Moreover the available alternatives were mostly men no more likely than he to delegate. Admiral Wemyss, installed by Geddes as Deputy First Sea Lord, had so little to do that he proposed to resign. Instead, on Christmas Eve, Geddes dismissed Jellicoe and offered Wemyss his place. The characteristically blunt manner in which the Navy's greatest living officer was dismissed caused great offence, and the junior sea lords even threatened resignation, but Geddes was not the man to relinquish his undoubted prerogative.[30]

There can be little doubt that he was right in his choice. Sir Rosslyn Wemyss was in no sense as great a sea commander as Jellicoe, but his limited talents were exactly what the Admiralty required. He was neither a centraliser by temperament nor a technical expert by profession. He happily delegated the routine work to his subordinates, and he had both the judgement to choose good men to serve him, and the courage to support them without interference. As a sophisticated and statesmanlike leader, a Francophile and a friend of the King, he was well equipped to lead the Navy in the closing stages of a coalition war. Wemyss's new approach was an immediate success; "decisions were now reached quickly and with everybody's knowledge, whereas before the rage for secrecy had resulted in confusion, overlapping and clumsy work."[31]

Thus at long last, in the final year of the war, the Admiralty arrived at an effective machinery for planning and directing war. Three and a half years and the loss of very many ships and lives had been required to rediscover and re-interpret in new circumstances the old truisms, on which the Navy's whole administrative system had for two centuries been based, that the functions of command and direction on the one hand, and of supply and sustenance on the other, are distinct but inseparable, and that neither can flourish, or even survive, without the other. The experience of going to war almost devoid of an effective head might have been fatal for the country but for the Navy's undiminished courage, its enormous numerical advantage, and the follies of its enemies.

In the other aspect of its responsibilities, by contrast, the Admiralty entered the Great War remarkably well equipped, and rose during it to strengths never equalled before or since. The administrative work taken over from the old Navy Board, which had come to dominate the Admiralty, was the one thing it did well. The ancient tradition of efficiency within the Admiralty Office, allied to the technical drive and enthusiasm of the Fisher era, created a remarkable combination. It has already been remarked how the Navy was in effect a society in miniature, a comprehensive, centrally directed society quite unlike the nation at large. This made it uniquely qualified to wage the first total war in modern history. The Cabinet scarcely interfered with the economic and social life of the nation before 1916, and the War Office, which was neither an operational headquarters nor responsible for much of the army's supplies, interfered still less with the army. The Admiralty, as the only comprehensive and competent body attuned to the needs of modern war, acquired responsibilities far beyond the war at sea. By 1917 the whole merchant fleet and the entire shipbuilding, ship-repairing and marine engine industry was under direct Admiralty control. Many enterprises, including torpedo factories, collieries, powder works and the largest oil company, were owned by the Admiralty. At one time the Admiralty was assigned the entire anti-aircraft defence of Britain, because there was no-one else to do it. It mounted a land-based strategic air offensive against Germany, and it dispatched substantial land forces to the interior of vast continents. It was chiefly responsible for the development of armoured cars and tanks, it was in the forefront of aircraft development, and of course it controlled all supplies for the Navy itself, which alone required quantities unimaginable in the previous century. In 1904 it was estimated that on the outbreak of war the Royal Victoria Victualling Yard at Deptford had to dispatch to the fleet such items as 837,500 lbs. of biscuit, 85,190 gallons of rum and 11,010 lbs. of mustard, while the Director of Contracts was at once to purchase 600,000 lbs. of jam, 10,000 bottles of port (for hospital ships) and so on.[32]

Of all the hundreds of departments of the Admiralty, none epitomises this universility more than the Naval Intelligence Division and its remarkable Director, Admiral Sir Reginald Hall. Hall's almost legendary reputation has always been based on the intelligence work of his division, and undoubtedly his extraordinary achievements in this field deserve all their fame. Even more remarkable, however, is the comprehensiveness of Hall's approach. If the Admiralty felt it could do almost anything, Hall felt N.I.D. could do more. Nothing was too great or too small for him, whether it was setting up a national postal censorship, treating for peace with Turkey (in each case without the knowledge of either the Cabinet or the Board) or stealing coal for his office. Even his agents hardly confined themselves to conventional spying; A. E. W. Mason in Spain was at one time reputed to be directly or indirectly employing over 40,000 men. The Cabinet turned to Hall to solve awkward problems ranging from victualling the Serbian army to breaking a dock strike in Buenos Aires. Most extraordinary of all was the affair of the Zimmerman Telegram—not so much that Room 40's cryptographers decrypted the signal which was instrumental in bringing the U.S.A. into the war, but that Balfour entrusted the Director of Naval Intelligence, not the Foreign Office, with the entire management of what must surely have been one of the most delicate diplomatic negotiations ever undertaken by a British Government.[33]

The war forced on the Admiralty, always a conservative body, many painful adjustments. The experienced clerks grew fewer as the number of staff rose, until by 1918 less than ten per cent had been in the Office in 1914. The numbers had by then increased from two thousand to about ten thousand, spread throughout buildings of different sorts in all parts of London. In 1914 the garden was built over, and a range of unsightly hutments, called "Murray's Mansions" after the Deputy Secretary, were erected on the roof. The clerks were organized into three watches, having one day a week off, while the senior officials took it in turns to sleep in the Office, and had no time off at all. The Deputy and Assistant Chiefs of Naval Staff likewise slept and ate in the building.

In the early part of the war the habits of a peaceful century faded only slowly, and the Admiralty, though busy, remained a relatively placid world. Air raids were initially a relief—an old messenger went around with a bell giving the alarm, and everyone went up onto the roof to watch the zeppelins, while Mr Perrin the librarian manned his anti-aircraft gun on top of the Admiralty Arch. The Assistant Secretary's duties still included allocating turtle soup to the Board, and the Deputy Secretary had to worry about the plumbing in Admiralty House. Churchill complained that the water came from the taps so odd a colour that he "dyed daily in his bath". Sir Oswyn Murray, having applied in vain to the Office of Works, replied that "salvation would have to be by faith as 'Works' were unable to help him."[34]

More unsettling than any air raid was the advent of women to the Admiralty. Before the war their Lordships had strenuously resisted a Treasury proposal to employ women typists instead of highly-paid boy clerks, concluding their case, according to tradition, with the ringing declaration that "their Lordships cannot conceal their decided preference for the boys". War, however, is no respecter of taste. Sir Reginald Hall and Sir John Parry, the Hydrographer, were the first to introduce women, and soon others followed. The first "lady typewriters" were securely locked in a guarded room, and the Board agitated for some time (though not, perhaps, entirely seriously) over whether women might be allowed into the Compass Department, at the risk of the steel ribs of their corsets upsetting the compasses and deranging the Navy's navigation.[35]

"Robed in the august authority of naval tradition and armed with the fullest authority available," wrote Churchill of the Admiralty in 1914, "the Board of Admiralty wielded unchallenged power". Unchallenged it was, but not necessarily unchallengeable, nor properly exercised. By the end of the war the Naval Staff had grown to 336 officers in twelve divisions, yet they had only just attained a suitable organization to control naval operations, and the "intellectual capital to float an efficient staff" was still in short supply. On the administrative side the Admiralty wielded a power which was hardly justifiable. Its unique fitness for modern war had allowed it to build a state within a state, but it remained unwilling to co-operate with the War Office or be directed by the Cabinet. It was one thing for Sir Oswyn Murray to use his initiative in 1914 in a matter technically requiring Parliamentary sanction, quite another for the Board to mount a strategic bombing offensive from France without informing the War Office or the General Staff. The days when war could safely be left to service ministries, especially those reluctant to submit to Cabinet control, were over by 1918 if they had ever existed. In the new wars the armed forces were but the "cutting edge of a mechanism which includes every single Department of State", and the characteristic instrument of control was the inter-departmental committee. The Admiralty's independence, which it believed to be inherited from remote antiquity, was in fact the novel product of an age of peace and uninterested Cabinets, and a world war forced the government to regain control of its wayward subordinate. Kitchener's concession in 1916 of a real rôle to the Chief of the Imperial General Staff, and the Admiralty reforms of 1917, spelled the end of the old dominance of Service ministers. In effect, the First Sea Lord and the

C.I.G.S. were now commanders-in-chief, backed by staffs able to give effect to their commands and support them in the formation of policy. Cabinets could with profit treat directly with them, as they had done in the eighteenth century when political admirals sat in the Cabinet. The Cabinet itself now had a staff to assist it in co-ordinating all aspects of policy, and the seamless web of committees of the Cabinet, the Committee of Imperial Defence and the service ministries bound all the disparate aspects of national defence into a whole. The magnificent independence and self-sufficiency of the Admiralty was an anachronism, and the Board, as a Board, was to be almost as completely eclipsed as it had been under William III. More accurately, perhaps, the Board, especially in time of war, functioned very much like the Navy Board, and with like duties, while the Chiefs of the Naval Staff, as heirs of the old Admiralty, planned and directed naval operations. In spite of its enormously increased size and scope, the Admiralty at the end of the Great War was no longer the autonomous body it had been at the beginning, but a part of a national scheme of defence to which all its power was in the end subordinated.[36]

NOTES

1 Murray, I, 14.
2 Hough, *First Sea Lord,* 189-190. Mackay, *Fisher,* 211, 335. Marder, *Dreadnought to Scapa Flow* [*DSF*] I, 16; *Fear God & Dread Nought* [*FGDN*] II, 17.
3 Roskill, *Hankey* I, 66. Marder, *DSF* I, 29-36; *FGDN* I, 243-247; II, 22.
4 Mackay, *Fisher,* 185, 189, 315. Kemp, *Fisher MSS* I, xxvi. Marder, *DSF* I, 81; *FGDN* I, 82-83; II, 37, 88.
5 Marder, *FGDN* I, 217; II, 15, 18, 59, 109, 477-478. Haggie, JCH VIII, 114-117, 130. Marder, *DSF* I, 332-333. Mackay, *Fisher,* 256-260, 297, 323. Dewar, *Aspects of Organisation,* 5. Schurman, 123. Kemp, II, 317.
6 Kemp, I, 2.
7 Johnson, 33-34, 41, 51, 80. *Ante,* p. 118. d'Ombrain, *War Machinery,* 36, 40-66. Marder, *FGDN* I, 279.
8 d'Ombrain, 157. Marder, *DSF* I, 385-390; II, 191-196. Haggie, 124.

9 Roskill, *Hankey* I, 79. Kemp, II, 317. Fremantle, *Naval Career*, 150. Haggie, 123. *Hankey* I, 33, 39.

10 Marder, *DSF* I, 198, 211-213. Bradford, *Wilson*, 141.

11 Marder, *DSF*, I, 242-245. Johnson, 114-115. Ehrman, *Cabinet Government*, 46-47. Hankey I, 78-82.

12 Johnson, 116. Marder, DSF I, 246-247, 253. Churchill, *World Crisis*, 240.

13 Ehrman, *Cabinet Government*, 46. Marder, *DSF* I, 247-248, 258, 265-266.

14 Ehrman, *Cabinet Government*, 48. Marder, *DSF* I, 265-266; II, 37; V, 314-315. Schurman, 126. Corelli Barnett, *The Swordbearers* (London, 1963), 119. Dewar, *Aspects of Organisation*, 5.

15 Marder, *DSF* I, 267-270; *FGDN* II, 401. Jack, P&P XXXIX, 139. Roskill, *Naval Air Service* I, 5.

16 Ehrman, *Cabinet Government*, 55-56. Murray, X, 335-336. Marder, *DSF* II, 38, 225-226. Churchill, 241.

17 King-Hall, *Naval Life*, 71. Marder, *FGDN* II, 412; *DSF* II, 270-271, 303. Roskill, *Hankey* I, 175. James, *Eyes of the Navy*, 82-89. Ehrman, *Cabinet Government*, 63.

18 Wells, "Naval Intelligence", 123-124, 130. Marder, *DSF* II, 37, 40, 51-53, 92; IV, 135; V, 314-315. Dewar, *Navy from Within*, 248-249. Barnett, 119. Sweetman, "Coronel", 87. Patterson, *Jellicoe MSS* I, 108, 127, 131, 237. Kemp, II, 116.

19 Ewing, *Man of Room 40*, 174. Wells, 125-131. Marder, *DSF* III, 42, 152.

20 Marder, *DSF* II, 37, 92, 299-300; III, 153; IV, 266; V, 60. Halpern, *Mediterranean Naval Situation*, 10-11. Beesly, *Very Special Intelligence*, 7. Hoy, *40 P.B.*, 8. James, *Great Seaman*, 141, 143. Kemp, II, 230-231.

21 Roskill, *Air Service* I, xiii. Marder, *DSF* II, 298-299; III, 280-283. Wells, 130 Roskill, *Hankey* I, 253, 315.

22 Marder, *DSF* III, 288-289; IV, 54-56.

23 Marder, *DSF* IV, 57, 114. Kemp, II, xiii, 116, 124-126. Dewar, *Navy from Within*, 242. Roskill, *Hankey* I, 253, 381.

24 Marder, *DSF* IV, 110-112, 172.

25 Roskill, *Hankey* I, 381-382, 409. Marder, *DSF* IV, 174, 177, 267.

26 Marder, *DSF* IV, 215. Roskill, *Hankey* I, 411; *Air Service* I, 157.

27 Marder, *DSF* IV, 174-178, 219-222. Kemp, II, 211. Murray, VIII, 96; X, 337-338. Walker, 126. *Hankey* II, 652-655.

28 Marder, *DSF* IV, 178, 215.

29 Marder, *DSF* IV, 134-135, 177, 224n.23. Kemp, II, 120. Dewar, *Navy from Within*, 238.

30 Marder, *DSF* IV, 325-340. Roskill, *Hankey* I, 447. Kemp II, 120. Wemyss, *Life & Letters*, 364-366.

31 Marder, *DSF* V, 4-10. Wemyss, 368-371.

32 Ehrman, *Cabinet Government*, 63. Murray, I, 15. Roskill, *Air Service* I, 166. Jones, *Strategic Bombing*, 39-41, 56, 79, 110. B. H. Liddell Hart, *The Tanks* (London, 1959, 2 vols.) I, 19, 29-35. ADM 116/3057.

33 James, *Eyes of the Navy*, 40-42, 63, 107-109, 143, 159. Hoy, 59.

34 Walker, 94, 109, 114, 128, 141. Murray, *Civil Servant*, 89-90. Fremantle, 239.

35 ADM 116/1297, which does not, alas, support the traditional wording. Sir Archibald Day, *The Admiralty Hydrographic Service 1795-1919* (London, 1967), 291. Walker, III.

36 Churchill, 239. Roskill, *Naval Policy* I, 127. Dewar, *Navy from Within,* 229. Murray, *Civil Servant,* 92. Roskill, *Air Service* I, 272. Ehrman, *Cabinet Government,* 110, 86. Howard, *Central Organisation of Defence*, 5.

CHAPTER NINE

BOARDS OF ADMIRALTY 1919-1964

First Lords:

20th July 1917	Sir Eric Geddes
14th January 1919	Walter Long
14th February 1921	Arthur, Viscount Lee
25th October 1922	Leopold Amery
23rd January 1924	Frederic Thesiger, Viscount Chelmsford
7th November 1924	William Bridgeman, later Viscount Bridgeman
8th June 1929	Albert Alexander
26th August 1931	Sir Austen Chamberlain
9th November 1931	Sir Bolton Eyres-Monsell, later Viscount Monsell
12th June 1936	Sir Samuel Hoare
28th May 1937	Alfred Duff Cooper
27th October 1938	James, Earl Stanhope
3rd September 1939	Winston Churchill
16th May 1940	Albert Alexander
29th May 1945	Brendan Bracken
4th August 1945	Albert Alexander
7th October 1946	George, Viscount Hall
30th May 1951	Francis, Lord Pakenham
5th November 1951	James Thomas, later Viscount Cilcennin
3rd September 1956	Quintin Hogg, Viscount Hailsham
17th January 1957	George Douglas-Hamilton, Earl of Selkirk
19th October 1959	Peter, Lord Carrington
21st October 1963	George, Earl Jellicoe

First Sea Lords:

10th January 1918	Sir Rosslyn Wemyss
1st November 1919	David, Earl Beatty
30th July 1927	Sir Charles Madden
30th July 1930	Sir Frederick Field
21st January 1933	Sir Ernle Chatfield, later Baron Chatfield
17th November 1938	Sir Roger Backhouse
15th June 1939	Sir Dudley Pound
15th October 1943	Sir Andrew Cunningham
10th June 1946	Sir John Cunningham
6th September 1948	Bruce, Lord Fraser
20th December 1951	Sir Rhoderick McGrigor
18th April 1955	Louis, Earl Mountbatten

1st May 1959	Sir Charles Lambe
23rd May 1960	Sir Caspar John
9th August 1963	Sir David Luce

Permanent Secretaries:

7th August 1917	Sir Oswyn Murray*
10th July 1936	Sir Archibald Carter
5th December 1940	Sir Henry Markham
8th January 1947	Sir John Lang
1st April 1961	Sir Clifford Jarrett
20th February 1964	A. L. M. Cary

*From 31st October 1921 the Secretary was a full member of the Board, holding office by patent.

CHAPTER NINE

A Multitude of Counsellors

"It is not too much to say that during the first half of this century the United Kingdom was defended by inter-departmental committees."

Michael Howard[1]

THE Great War ended at an unfortunate time for the Admiralty. Very late, almost too late in the day, it had at last learnt to handle the problems of a world war, and now it was faced with the problems — if anything, still more intractable — of peace. The economic troubles of the country during the next twenty years were to reduce the fighting services to the position they had occupied for so much of Queen Victoria's reign; the delinquent step-children of the state, seen with approval but heard with impatience, reproached and punished for their spendthrift ways, denied a real voice in the counsels of the realm, even a real rôle in its defence. For men who had known, and had been taught to expect, the unprecedented luxury of public support without public criticism, this was a bitter and unexpected blow.

The problems of the Navy at the end of the war were acute and immediate. In the first place, it was still at war in the Baltic against the Bolsheviks, and equally heavily committed against the Turks in the Mediterranean. By April 1919 40,000 men had not yet been demobilized — and they, moreover, the least dispensable, and consequently longest-serving. There were mutinies or near-mutinies among the forces in Russia. The Board had to contend with Cabinets from which it could obtain no clear naval policy, except the urgent and overriding need for economy. The Admiralty early accepted that a "One Power Standard" was the best that could be hoped for. It fought, with a determination creditable to a body so recently and so hardly convinced, against any attempt to abolish or emasculate the Naval Staff, which in 1919 was re-organized so that in its smaller peacetime form its eight divisions bore a more logical and coherent relation to one another.[2]

At the end of the war neither the First Lord nor the First Sea Lord was eager to continue in office. Geddes wished to return to the Ministry of Transport, which he did in January 1919, and Wemyss looked forward to a dignified retirement post as a suitable reward for his labours. Meanwhile Sir David Beatty fretted at his moorings in the Firth of Forth, anxious to relieve him. When an admiral has had his Union Flag at the maintop as an Admiral of the Fleet commanding at sea, as Beatty had before the Grand Fleet was dissolved in April 1919 (the first Admiral of the Fleet at sea since Anson in 1761), there is no further ambition afloat, and he might have taken Wemyss's place earlier if a certain streak of vanity in both men had not made needless difficulties. Moreover, Wemyss wished to complete the valuable reforms which he had in train (notably a long-overdue increase in pay for officers and men), and there were political obstacles to the change. Finally, however, on 1st November 1919, Sir David now earl, Beatty became First Sea Lord.[3]

Like Jellicoe, Beatty as a sea commander inspired great devotion among his officers and men, and some controversy among detached observers. Although, or because, this handsome, wealthy and accomplished man at times seemed to be playing the Prince Rupert of the twentieth century, there were misgivings about his handling of his ships at sea. Perhaps, given the chance, he might have led the Grand Fleet to victory; there is no doubt that he was an outstanding First Sea Lord in a very demanding time for the Navy. He had considerable intellectual gifts, and was a skilled and redoubtable debater. "A tremendous and impressive personality . . . who had in him some elements of a bounder", he could deal with politicians in their own language. "You are the only First Sea Lord I have known in my twenty-six years experience," Sir Maurice Hankey, the Secretary of the Cabinet, told him, "who could really talk on even terms to the highest Cabinet Ministers and stand up to them in argument". For eight years Beatty dominated the Admiralty and guided the Navy through a period of acute difficulty.[4]

The Washington Naval Treaty of 1920 and the recommendations of the Geddes Committee on National Expenditure in 1921 (the "Geddes

Axe") presented Beatty with immediate crises. There can be few less agreeable times to lead a service than in a period of enforced and drastic reductions, and Beatty had to do it with little political support. Walter Long fell ill in his second year in office, Lord Lee's "chief interest had always been in the field of the arts", and L. C. M. S. Amery, "an ardent and devoted imperialist of the old school", lasted only as long as Bonar Law's government, which was fifteen months. Lord Chelmsford, whom Ramsay MacDonald appointed, was out with him in ten months. Four political heads, none of them of the first rank in politics, and only one particularly keen on the Navy, had succeeded one another in the first five years of Beatty's term of office. He outlasted them, he outmatched them in abilities and strength of character, and his constitutional standing, even in peacetime, was growing at their expense. It has been remarked how the machinery of government established by 1918 allowed the Cabinet to deal directly with the professional heads of the three services. The creation in 1923 of the Chiefs of Staff Committee (of the Committee of Imperial Defence) gave institutional form to the new realities. The natural advisers on service questions, to whom the Cabinet most easily turned, were not the service ministers now, but the Chiefs of Staff.[5]

This made it all the more important that First Sea Lords should be men of ability and strength, and all the more unfortunate that Beatty's two successors were not. Sir Charles Madden had considerable intellectual gifts, but lacked the force to project them; Sir Frederick Field was "without doubt the most colourless First Sea Lord of our period". On the other hand W. C. Bridgeman, First Lord under Baldwin from 1924 to 1929, was a conspicuously honest and guileless man, by no means without ability, and deservedly popular.[6]

Under this varied leadership the Admiralty of the 1920s struggled with the problems of peace and retrenchment. It needed all the continuity it could provide, because both Board members and other naval officers changed frequently. Between 1920 and 1925 there were five First Lords, seven Parliamentary Secretaries, six Civil Lords, and eighteen sea lords. Between 1900 and 1925 there had been thirteen First Lords, ten First Sea Lords, and twelve Controllers. Of the two hundred naval officers in the Admiralty in December 1925, only sixty had been there two years before. This made the Secretary's Department, which co-ordinated the work of all the departments of the Admiralty, of peculiar importance. More than forty departments, many of them of great size, divided the Admiralty's diverse but unified responsibilities. There were Directors of Naval Construction, of Electrical Engineering, of Naval Ordnance, of Torpedoes and Mining, of the Signal Department and the Compass Department, of Naval Equipment, of Contracts, of Dockyards, of Naval Stores, of Naval Intelligence, of Scientific Research, of Victualling, of Statistics, of Mobilization, of Naval Recruiting, and of the several divisions of the Naval Staff. There was the Engineer in Chief and the Civil Engineer in Chief, the Chief Superintendent of Armament Supply and the Chief Inspector of Naval Ordnance, the Hydrographer and the Chaplain of the Fleet, the Medical Director-General and the Admiral commanding Reserves, the Paymaster Director-General and the Adjutant-General of the Royal Marines. The list is not exhaustive, but it serves to illustrate the remarkable size and scope of even the shrunken Admiralty of the 1920s.[7]

From the experiences of the war the Admiralty had learned much of administrative value. It was able to achieve substantial economics and efficiency, as well as eliminating a legal anomaly by merging the Accountant-General's Department with the Secretariat. It had learned a skill in costing which stood it in good stead when ordnance and warship builders became so few that tenders had to be accepted in conditions of near monopoly. The great numbers of naval officers in the Admiralty, and the crucial rôle of the clerks in providing continuity, made it doubly important that the two should associate smoothly, and the Admiralty was able to create "a team of civil servants and sailors working together in happy mutual trust and confidence" — a very different case from the other service ministries.[8]

Much of the credit for these achievements belongs with Sir Oswyn Murray, Secretary from 1917 until his death in 1936. Murray was a man of great intellectual powers, but the quality which most impressed his colleagues was what the Greeks called επιεικεια — "It was extraordinarily difficult to find good reasons for differing from him". For a man of such strength of character and cogency of argument to be so generally beloved is itself a remarkable tribute. For twenty years successive Boards depended on him as their "wise and trusted friend".[9]

The Admiralty Arch soon after its completion

G.L.C. Photograph Library

Sir Eric Geddes as Controller in 1917, wearing his uniform
National Portrait Gallery

Sir Rosslyn Wemyss in 1918 *National Portrait Gallery*

Sir David Beatty in 1919 *National Portrait Gallery*

The Entrance Hall of the Admiralty in 1934

G.L.C. Photograph Library

An Admiralty office: Room 57 O.B. in 1934

G.L.C. Photograph Library

Sir Oswyn Murray, in one of the old-fashioned collars he always wore *National Portrait Gallery*

The Citadel as it appears to-day — *G.L.C. Photograph Library*

Earl Mountbatten in 1955, the year he became First Sea Lord *National Portrait Gallery*

It is instructive to consider Murray's position compared to that of some of his great predecessors. He was the key functionary in a vast and complex organization which he, more than any other man, had to understand and animate. On the smallest detail of administration or the highest question of policy he was the Board's first adviser. His practical power far exceeded that of Burchett or Stephens and has been equalled only by Pepys. Yet he undoubtedly stood lower in the body politic than any Secretary of the eighteenth century. They had been political officers with patronage at their disposal, and he was simply a civil servant. For this reason alone, Cleveland and Stephens had enjoyed a place in the social and political world more resembling Beatty's than Murray's.

Of all the Secretary's preoccupations, none was more important or more onerous than the struggle against the Treasury. Nearly a century had passed since Boards of Admiralty had been able to spend money without reference to any central control, and no responsible person in the Admiralty looked for the return of such freedom, least of all in the economic climate of the 1920s. Nevertheless, the methods of the Treasury were not ideally calculated to win co-operation. Its "petty inquisitorial interrogations", its calculated delays, its habit of setting up highly partisan committees to give a judicial colour to preconceived opinions, were resented as unfair and underhand, and so temperate an observer as Lord Chatfield was moved to compare the Treasury with the Gestapo. In order to defend the Navy from these onslaughts, inessentials were abandoned wholesale, even extending to Mall House, the First Sea Lord's residence, which was turned over to offices in 1931.[10]

Nevertheless, the Admiralty between the wars was not solely concerned with grim economics, not taken up entirely with grave and serious matters. In 1921 the Board found time to consider the pay of the Library cat, and the delicate question of whether she were a rating, a civil servant, or an unpensionable employee; Murray particularly recommending the question to the Financial Secretary "in accordance with the direction of his first predecessor in Office, Mr. Samuel Pepys, who records in his Diary giving orders that 'not even a cat should swing in the Navy Office but he should know it'."[11]

Twenty years of peace and severe economy made a vigorous test of the lessons learned during the Great War. The natural tendency, perhaps, would have been to relax into the peacetime routine, to emasculate or abandon the Naval Staff, and forget once again the need for so large an institution to have a thinking brain. "The continual perusal of dockets, telegrams and reports dealing with a wide variety of subjects acts like a drug. It dulls the perceptive faculties and paralyses power of criticism and selection behind a deceptive façade of hard work". This fatal error the Admiralty under Beatty and Murray creditably resisted. The Naval Staff, wrote Murray, is the "Alpha and Omega of the Admiralty alphabet", while *The Child's Guide to the Admiralty*, prepared in 1941 for newcomers to the Admiralty, described the Naval Staff as "the dynamo of the naval war machine". For men trained by Fisher, with his belief that a staff was useful, if at all, only to ameliorate the effects of a fool as First Sea Lord, this was a rapid reversal of opinion.[12]

The firmness with which the Admiralty preserved the lessions of the war was one of the factors which saved it from disaster during the unhappy decade of the 1930s. It was a period of exceptionally weak political and, often, naval leadership. Cabinets lacked the strength, or interest, to form coherent naval policies, and hardly considered the fleet except as a source of economies. A. V. Alexander, the Labour First Lord from 1929 to 1931, was a colourless man, apt to follow the will of men stronger than himself, and determined to keep any of them off the Board. "The result was to produce perhaps the weakest Board of Admiralty of all time". Moreover a number of promising potential First Sea Lords died young or were invalided during the 1930s, further reducing the field. From 1931 to 1935 Ramsay MacDonald's National Government excluded the First Lord from the Cabinet, for the first time since Queen Anne's reign. In 1931, three months after this innovation, with an inexperienced First Lord, Sir Austen Chamberlain, and a weak and sickly First Sea Lord, Sir Frederick Field, and with Sir Oswyn Murray on leave, the Board's inept handling of the May Committee's report led directly to the Invergordon Mutiny. This was unquestionably the low point of the Navy's, and the Admiralty's, fortunes in the twentieth century, but from the disaster much was learnt. The Board made a conscious effort to regain contact with the lower deck, and to remove the "feeling in the Navy that the Admiralty was a thing apart from the sailor, a body that wore top hats and was their permanent enemy". The new First Sea Lord, Sir Ernle Chatfield, as soon as he came in 1933, arranged for the Board to go on its tours of inspection in uniform, the civilian members being clothed in a species of yachting rig. Sir Bolton Eyres-Monsell, who became First Lord when Chamberlain resigned after Invergordon, had in fact the distinction of being a naval officer, albeit long retired, the first since the duke of Northumberland in 1852.[13]

Monsell and Chatfield gave the Admiralty the leadership of which it stood badly in need. Though scarcely a politician of the first rank, Monsell had skill, tact and patience, and his knowledge of and loyalty to the Navy were not in question. Chatfield, in spite of his deceptively quiet manner, had the finest mind and the strongest character of any First Sea Lord since Beatty. As Monsell remained in office until 1936, and Chatfield until 1938, they were able to give the Admiralty firm and stable leadership during a crucial period. Though the general public were as yet hardly aware of it, the likelihood of war was growing. Slowly at first, then more rapidly as the decade advanced, money was becoming available for rebuilding the fleet and strengthening the Admiralty. The War Registry was expanded and re-organized in 1934 and 1937, a register of scientists was established on whose services the Admiralty could call, and the wireless network strengthened.[14] Far more important than any of these, however, was the establishment in 1937 by Admiral Sir William James, the Deputy Chief of Naval Staff, of the Operational Intelligence Centre. James was a former head of Room 40, and he was determined that never again would the conduct of naval war suffer from the disastrous weaknesses which he had known. The O.I.C. was the successor of the former War Room, but it was much more than a central plot, dominated though it was by its huge brilliantly-lit plotting table. It was the centre to which came all intelligence and information, and from which came all operational orders. It represented the physical embodiment of that unified central control of the war at sea towards which the Admiralty had been groping in 1918.[15]

The last years before the war were once again a time of weakness for the Board. Three First Lords succeeded one another in as many years, while Chatfield was relieved by Sir Roger Backhouse, a fanatical centralizer whose health broke down before he had been a year in office. The deaths of so many candidates for his place left a poor field in 1939, and only one man seemed an obvious choice, Sir Dudley Pound. When war was declared in September 1939 and W. S. Churchill resumed the office he had left twenty-four years earlier, Pound had less than three months' experience. Moreover, Sir Oswyn Murray, the strength and stay of so many Boards, had died in 1936, and his successor, Sir Archibald Carter, brought in from the India Office, was neither liked nor admired.[16]

The situation in 1939 set the tone of the Admiralty for much of the war. As an administrative organization it remained excellent, and it had newly acquired an efficient means of directing the war at sea, but at the top its leadership was not as united or as settled as it might have been. Churchill as First Lord, in spite of having been instrumental in forming the first Naval Staff in 1912, never learned to trust or work with a staff. Perhaps because he unconsciously associated them with their predecessors of 1914, he consistently under-rated, ignored and misused his staff officers. He was not above dismissing those whose advice conflicted with his own ideas, and he interfered in operations in a way more characteristic of intrigue than command. In the circumstances of war in 1940, it was unquestionably irresponsible to maintain private channels of communication with flag officers at sea by which to circumvent the Admiralty. Moreover Churchill did not tolerate strong men around him. Pound was the embodiment of exactly those faults which had been so disastrous at the Admiralty in the earlier war. He was an obsessive centralizer who worked far too hard, yet lacked the character to defend his staff against Churchill's onslaughts. He suffered from several serious and painful illnesses, including a tumour on the brain which affected his concentration. He was a humourless, narrow man, "a driver rather than a leader", with none of the breadth of intellect and experience which might have helped him to stand up to Churchill on the one hand, and leave commanders at sea to make their own decisions on the other.[17]

When Churchill became Prime Minister the position of the Admiralty changed little. As his own Minister of Defence, he continued to interfere with operations (using the Admiralty War Registry for all his private signal traffic), and Pound did not prevent him. The new First Lord, A. V. Alexander, was nicely chosen to provide stolid administrative efficiency (and political balance) with little risk of a challenge to Churchill's authority. Indeed, the constitutional and personal position of the First Lord had now sunk to a lower position than ever before. The Cabinet, dominated by the Prime Minister, dealt directly with the Joint Chiefs of Staff. The service ministers were left out of the inner councils of the war and treated simply as administrators. The War Cabinet was divided into Operational and Supply Committees, just like the Admiralty Board of 1917 to 1919, with the Chiefs of Staff on the former directing the war, and their ministers dancing ineffectual attendance. The Committee of Imperial Defence Secretariat at Storey's Gate, which filled the triple rôle of Cabinet Office, Ministry of Defence and Prime Minister's Office, connected the Prime Minister, the Chiefs of Staff and the service staffs. Among these committees, the Board of Admiralty played only a minor part, and the status of the First Lord stood accordingly low. It remained central to the vast organization of supply and administration, but as a Board it had little to do with operations any longer. In all but name, it was another Navy Board.[18] The Naval Staff which actually directed the war at sea, and the Operational Intelligence Centre which was the brain of the whole organization, were faced with unparalleled opportunities, and problems. Never before had war been fought on so vast a scale, with such exact information. By teleprinter from every corner of the world an unceasing flow of information came into the unhealthy but secure fastnesses beneath the Citadel ("Lenin's Tomb", as it was immediately renamed) where the O.I.C. moved in 1940. Above all, the work of the Government Code and Cypher School at Bletchley Park provided the Navy with decyphered texts of many of the most informative signals of the enemy. No leader in war had ever had such good information to work on as Pound had from late in 1914. He has often been reproached for interfering excessively with commanders at sea, but in the light of what we now know, it may seem that the real fault lay not in direction from the centre in itself, but in entrusting so great a responsibility to a sick man, temperamentally unable to delegate or properly to use a staff. The disaster to convoy PQ 17, often adduced as an example of needless meddling, now appears in a rather different light; as a decision not inexcusable in principle, but taken with too little thought and consultation. With the priceless information from the Enigma machine, both Churchill and Pound were presented with opportunities which they were apt to abuse. In the words of Sir John Tovey, Commander-in-Chief of the Home Fleet from 1940 to 1943, who knew about the Enigma traffic and was no immoderate opponent of Admiralty control, "WSC as Prime Minister is magnificent and unique, but as a strategist and tactician he is liable to be most dangerous".[19]

When Sir Dudley Pound died, Churchill had no such pliant successor to hand. It was Mr Alexander, to his credit, who insisted that Sir Andrew Cunningham was the essential choice, a man whose force of character Churchill had already learned to respect, if not to fear. "Like the giant panda," wrote one of his subordinates, "he had endearing qualities, but he could bite you if you got too close". Another wrote of "his astonishing decentralisation and reliance on his staff". A man with the moral courage both to trust and to protect his subordinates was very much better fitted by nature to guide the Navy in a modern war, and to serve such a master as Churchill, than Pound had been. If Cunningham or someone like him had been appointed in 1939 there seems little doubt that the Navy would have suffered less during the war, and Churchill's reputation after it, than they have done.[20]

When the World War ended in 1945 the Admiralty had grown to a size and complexity undreamed of by its predecessors. Entire departments had spread, not only from the Admiralty buildings, but from Whitehall and even from London. The Controller's departments had settled at Bath, and the Hydrographer yet further afield, in Taunton. Yet in spite of its numbers, and in spite of the continual change of its naval members, the Admiralty remained remarkably cohesive and preserved an identity quite distinct from other ministries. Compared to the War Office or the Air Ministry, there were relatively few service officers, and they were closely integrated with the clerks. It was remarked that in inter-service committees the Admiralty was happy to be represented either by a civilian or by a naval officer, rather than both as was the practice of the other services, and that its representatives were usually much more junior than their counterparts, reflecting the extent to which the Admiralty delegated its business. "There is little doubt," considered an outside observer, "that the Admiralty is the most effective of the three service headquarters". Another described it as "an absolutely first-class organization, in a class by itself". One Secretary for War paid rueful tribute to the Admiralty's effectiveness: "The Navy is like the Russians. It does not have to go to war because it always gets what it wants without a struggle". The Admiralty had a strong sense of its own history and identity, clinging jealously to its traditions. When a correspondent in *The Times* complained that the Admiralty alone had not half-masted its flag on the death of King George VI, the Secretary replied magisterially that the flag, being a corporative and not a national or personal emblem, would stay close up "even in so untoward an event as the simultaneous demise of all My Lords".[21]

Yet the lessons of the war presaged exactly that untoward event. The only way to conduct great and complex operations had proved to be by joint-service headquarters, with a high degree of co-ordination between all arms. In the light of such experience, it was inconceivable that the three services should be allowed to go their separate ways in Whitehall. Though it was not at once clear how the national defences were to be re-organized, there could be no doubt in what direction things had to move. In 1946 the Committee of Imperial Defence was replaced by a Defence Committee of the Cabinet, with the C.I.D. Secretariat in Storey's Gate now formally named the Ministry of Defence. Lacking a staff, however, and lacking defined authority, the new Minister of Defence was "like one of the unhappier Merovingian Kings, without even a mayor of the Palace to pre-empt his non-existent powers".[22]

Like so many British constitutional shifts, the 1946 Ministry of Defence lasted longer than might have been expected, but in the aftermath of the Suez expedition the Minister was given definite powers to decide strategic priorities, powers which Mr Sandys used to the full. The powers of the Chairman of the Joint Chiefs of Staff were still carefully restricted.[23]

Behind this lay not only a natural fear of over-mighty subjects, but a specific unease. Earl Mountbatten became First Sea Lord in 1955, and was to be the next Chairman of the Chiefs of Staff. Many people in politics and the services viewed the prospect with apprehension, and had no desire to endow the post with too much power. But the unhappy compromise of 1958 soon revealed itself as a failure, and the necessity for change, no longer to be denied, only increased the strength of Mountbatten's position.

It is interesting to note how as its powers declined the Admiralty was able to throw up some remarkable First Sea Lords. Having already had Beatty and Chatfield in the space of thirty years, it was surely against probability to have another as great, or greater. Mountbatten's career might more plausibly be placed in the sixteenth century than the twentieth. His wealth and birth, his extraordinary energy and ability, his unique professional experience were in themselves enough to set him above most politicians and all naval officers, had he never served as a Supreme Commander and Viceroy of India. Little wonder that he was held by most politicians "in a respect bordering on awe". In the Admiralty he was known as "the Hound of the Battenbergs". He arrived in office with unequalled strength of character and of position, knowing what he wanted, and with the backing to achieve it. Wartime experience had convinced him that only a unified command and administration could match the demands of modern war. First he applied the ideas to overseas commands, then in 1962 came the proposal to abolish the service ministries and combine their functions in a single Ministry of Defence. A project to abolish the Roman Curia would hardly have met with less enthusiasm in the Vatican than Cmd. 2097, *The Central Organisation for Defence*, aroused in Whitehall. Even the unmatched political, professional and personal weight behind the Ministry of Defence scarcely sufficed to propel it down the ways.

This study is not the place, nor is the time yet ripe, to trace in detail the contest which raged throughout 1962 and 1963, and from which the new Ministry of Defence finally emerged. It is enough to say that on 31st March 1964 the Board of Admiralty met for the last time, its patent was surrendered, and its flag hauled down. On All Fools' Day the new Ministry officially assumed the charge of Her Majesty's ships and vessels, and the members of the Board resumed their former seats as the "Admiralty Board of the Defence Council", no longer Lords Commissioners, for the Queen had resumed the office of Lord Admiral into her own hands.[24]

Thus after three hundred and thirty-six years ended a unique and remarkable feature of the British governmental system. Devised as a temporary expedient to pay off the debts of a dead favourite, it had survived to become a venerable part of the constitution, preserving into the twentieth century the form at least, if not the substance, of a species of government peculiarly characteristic of the seventeenth. In many ways the Admiralty's antiquity was deceptive, for not only was it surprisingly modern in its outlook and methods, but its constitutional form was little more than a façade behind which the actual power, position and character of the Board changed repeatedly. Some Boards were composed of powerless sinecurists; other Boards, and certainly other First Lords, were able to dictate to the governments of the day. One thing was nearly constant, that only in times of extreme debility did the Board ever function as a Board, if by that is meant an assembly of equals taking collective decisions. The political authority of the First Lord, or the professional authority of the Senior Naval Lord, almost always dominated the Board and directed its policy. When the Admiralty was confined to its proper and original rôle of directing the fleet, the junior lords had little to do but sign their names occasionally, until improved communications and the wider scope of war increased the Admiralty's operational responsibilities, and bade fair to make them something like a naval staff. This prospect was extinguished by a century of peace, in which the Admiralty first absorbed, and then was absorbed by the Navy Board, and had to spend much of the twentieth century painfully rediscovering a mechanism for the central direction of naval war. By the end of its history the Board of Admiralty was in effect the functional, if not the lineal descendant of the Navy Board, and might have taken that name in the new organization if misplaced sentiment had not secured the preservation of the newer title. So in a sense the wheel came full circle, and a council of the marine assumed a structure and responsibilities not unlike those which Henry VIII had envisaged more than four hundred years before. The history of the Admiralty abounds in such paradoxes. No department of state survived so long, through so many metamorphoses and vicissitudes, as the Admiralty. When most of the great departments of state were born, it was already ancient, and yet it never lost a certain chameleon-like quality, ever-changing, and never quite matching its background. In spite, or perhaps because, of its strong regard for its own history, it neither became set in its own ways, nor easily adopted those of others. Monarchs and dynasties, statesmen and ministries came and went, the tides of war and revolution washed over and around, constantly altering but never submerging the Admiralty, and it survived them all, counter, original, spare and strange to the last.

NOTES

1 Howard, 5.
2 Roskill, *Naval Policy* I, 21, 103, 127-128, 142, 208.
3 Marder, *DSF* V, 199-218. Roskill, *Naval Policy* I, 42-43.
4 King-Hall, 222. Roskill, *Naval Policy* I, 44-46, 337.
5 Roskill, *Naval Policy* I, 30-33. Murray, X, 334. Ehrman, *Cabinet Government,* 109-110.
6 Roskill, *Naval Policy* I, 34-36, 46-48; II, 69-70.
7 Murray, IX, 219-226. ADM 1/10288, *Child's Guide to the Admiralty,* p. 12.
8 ADM 116/3344. Walker, 163. Murray, *Civil Servant,* 164. Lyon, 63. Nailor, "Military Bureacracy", 189. Chatfield, 185.
9 Marder, *DSF* V, 216; cf. Philippians IV, 5. Roskill, *Naval Policy* I, 209. Chatfield, *Navy & Defence*, 185; *It Might Happen Again*, 16, 63.
10 Roskill, *Naval Policy* I, 206-209. 454-455; II, 82. Chatfield, *It Might Happen Again*, 11. Murray, *Civil Servant,* 196.
11 ADM 1/9237.
12 Marder, *DSF* IV, 135. Dewar, *Navy from Within*, 296. Murray, X, 328. ADM 1/10288 p. 6. Marder, *FGDN* II, 412.
13 Till, 109. Roskill, *Navy Policy* I, 25, 36, 50; II, 79-80, 90-94, 122-123, 131-132, 462. Chatfield, *Navy and & Defence,* 85; *It Might Happen Again*, 52-53.
14 Roskill, *Naval Policy* I, 49; II, 125, 244, 338-339, 388.
15 Roskill, *Naval Policy* II, 388. Wells, 134. McLachlan, 54-56, 59, 107. Beesly, 9-23.
16 Marder, *DSF* IV, 28n.7. Roskill, *Naval Policy* II, 245, 462-465. Nailor, 193.
17 Roskill, *Churchill & the Admirals,* 94-95, 99, 101, 105, 116-117, 123, 237. Gretton, *Former Naval Person,* 198-199, 267. Roskill, *Naval Policy* II, 463-465. Viscount Cunningham, *A Sailor's Odyssey* (London, 1951), 584.
18 Roskill, *Naval Policy* I, 36; II, 339; *Churchill,* 265. Howard, 6. Ehrman, *Cabinet Government*, 127-128. Lewin, *Churchill as Warlord,* 34. Hans Daalder, *Cabinet Reform in Britain, 1914-1963* (Stanford, California, 1964), 175.

19 Roskill, *Naval Policy* II, 338, 448; *Churchill,* 130. McLachlan, 119-120. Beesly, *passim.*

20 Roskill, *Churchill,* 237. Warner, *Cunningham,* 274. S. W. C. Pack, *Cunningham the Commander* (London, 1974), 277.

21 Snyder, *Politics of Defence Policy,* 124-126, 170. Nailor, 180-181, 197-198. McLachlan, 57.

22 Howard, 7.

23 Howard, 9-11.

24 Howard, 11-18.

Bibliography

Abbreviations:

ADM	Admiralty records in the Public Record Office
AHR	American Historical Review
BIHR	Bulletin of the Institute of Historical Research
CHJ	Cambridge Historical Journal
EHR	English Historical Review
EcHR	Economic History Review
HLQ	Huntington Library Quarterly
JCH	Journal of Contemporary History
JMH	Journal of Modern History
MM	The Mariner's Mirror
NRS	Navy Records Society
PA	Public Administration
P&P	Past and Present

W. A. Aiken, "The Admiralty in Conflict and Commission", in *Essays in Honour of Wallace Notestein: Conflict in Stuart England,* ed. W. A. Aiken and B. D. Henning (London, 1960).

William Ashworth, "Economic Aspects of late Victorian Naval Administration", EcHR 2° XXII p. 491.

Cecil Aspinall-Oglander, *Admiral's Wife; The Life and Letters of Mrs Edward Boscawen, 1719-1761* (London, 1940).

Stanley Ayling, *The Elder Pitt, Earl of Chatham* (London, 1976). An important study of Pitt as a war minister.

G. E. Aylmer, *The King's Servants: The Civil Service of Charles I* (London, 1961).
The States' Servants: The Civil Service of the English Republic, 1649-1660 (London, 1973). Both of these learned and fascinating works are essential for an understanding of the place of the administrator in the society of their day.
"Attempts at Administrative Reform, 1625-1640", EHR LXXII p. 229. Treats of the nature and use of royal commissions in the time of Charles I.

G. R. Barnes and J. H. Owen (eds.), *The Private Papers of John, Earl of Sandwich* (London, 1932-8, 4 vols. NRS 69, 71, 75, 78). The importance of Sandwich as First Lord sufficiently emphasizes the importance of his papers.

C. J. Bartlett, *Great Britain and Sea Power, 1815-1853* (Oxford, 1963). The standard account of the period.

Daniel Baugh, *British Naval Administration in the Age of Walpole* (Princeton, New Jersey, 1966).

Naval Administration, 1715-1750 (London, 1977, NRS 120). A detailed and masterly study, with a selection of supporting documents.

Patrick Beesly, *Very Special Intelligence* (London, 1977). The work of the Operational Intelligence Centre during the Second World War, by one of its staff. This is one of the first works to reveal the existence of ULTRA.

J. E. D. Binney, *British Public Finance and Administration, 1774-1792* (Oxford, 1958). A subject not only fundamental to administrative history, but in this period of great political moment.

Sir Edward Bradford, *Life of Admiral of the Fleet Sir Arthur Knyvet Wilson* (London, 1923).

Sir J. H. Briggs, *Naval Administrations, 1827-1892* (London, 1897). Informative memoirs of a senior clerk, albeit naive and confessedly partisan.

J. H. Broomfield, "Lord Sandwich at the Admiralty Board: Politics and the British Navy, 1771-1778", MM LI p. 7.

C. D. Chandaman, *The English Public Revenue, 1660-1688* (Oxford, 1975). Not directly related to the Admiralty, but fundamental to all problems of naval administration.

Lord Chatfield, *The Navy and Defence* (London, 1942).

It Might Happen Again (London, 1947).

Two volumes of autobiography, the first naturally muted by the circumstances of 1942.

Viscount Chilston, *W. H. Smith* (London & Toronto, 1965).

W. S. Churchill, *The World Crisis, 1911-1915* (London, 1923). A political defence of his time as First Lord.

J. M. Collinge, *Navy Board Officials, 1660-1832* (London, Institute of Historical Research, 1978. No. VII of "Office holders in Modern Britain"). Invaluable not only for the list of officials, but for the introductory notes on the administrative history of the Board.

P. H. Colomb, *Memoirs of Sir Astley Cooper Key* (London, 1898). Almost the only informative life of a Victorian First Sea Lord.

M. E. Condon, "The Establishment of the Transport Board—A Subdivision of the Admiralty—4th July 1794", MM XLVIII p. 69.

Julian S. Corbett (ed.), *The Private Papers of George, second Earl Spencer* (London, 1913-14, 2 vols., NRS 46 & 48; continued by Richmond, q.v.).

Alan Cowpe, "The Royal Navy and the Whitehead Torpedo". In *Technical Change and British Naval Policy 1860-1939*, ed. B. McL. Ranft (London, 1977).

P. K. Crimmin, "Admiralty Relations with the Treasury, 1783-1806: The Preparation of Naval Estimates and the Beginnings of Treasury Control", MM LIII p. 63.
"The Financial and Clerical Establishment of the Admiralty Office, 1783-1806", MM LV p. 229.

Patrick Crowhurst, *The Defence of British Trade, 1689-1815* (Folkestone, 1977). Contains a mass of valuable material, scarcely digested.

C. S. L. Davies, "The Origin of the Navy Board under Henry VIII", EHR LXXX p. 268.

E. S. de Beer, "The Lord High Admiral and the Administration of the Navy", MM XIII p. 45.

A. C. Dewar, *On Certain Aspects of Organisation* (Kirkwall, 1917, privately printed).
"The Naval Administration of the Interregnum, 1641-59", MM XII p. 406.

K. G. B. Dewar, *The Navy from within* (London, 1939). Both Dewar brothers were trenchant and generally perceptive critics of the Admiralty, which is one reason why they did not rise high in the Service.

P. G. M. Dickson, *The Financial Revolution in England. A Study in the Development of Public Credit, 1688-1756* (London, 1967).

Nicholas D'Ombrain, *War Machinery and High Policy* (London, 1973). A tendentious but stimulating re-interpretation of the Committee of Imperial Defence.

John Ehrman, *The Navy in the War of William III, 1689-97* (Cambridge, 1953). A magisterial study, complete and satisfying.
"William III and the Emergence of a Mediterranean Naval Policy, 1692-4", CHJ IX p. 269.
Cabinet Government and War (Cambridge, 1958). An analysis of fundamental importance.

A. W. Ewing, *The Man of Room 40: The Life of Sir Alfred Ewing* (London, 1939).

S. E. Finer, "Patronage and the Public Service", PA XXX p. 329.

Sir Sydney Fremantle, *My Naval Career 1880-1928* (London, 1949).

Leslie Gardiner, *The British Admiralty* (Edinburgh, 1968). A collection of anecdotes rather than a serious history, and extremely unreliable in its facts, but nevertheless worth reading, especially for its account of the Admiralty and the Admiralty buildings in the recent past.

S. R. Gardiner and C. T. Atkinson (eds.), *Papers relating to the First Dutch War, 1652-54* (London, 1889-1930. 6 vols., NRS 13, 17, 30, 37, 41, 66).

Tom Glasgow, "Maturing of Naval Administration, 1556-1564", MM LVI p. 3.

Richard Glover, *Britain at Bay; Defence against Bonaparte 1803-14* (London, 1973).

G. S. Graham, *The Walker Expedition to Quebec, 1711* (London, 1953, NRS 94).

David Green, *Queen Anne* (London, 1970).

Sir Peter Gretton, *Former Naval Person* (London, 1968). Churchill's relations with the Navy; Roskill's treatment is more complete, but complements rather than replaces this.

Paul Haggie, "The Royal Navy and War Planning in the Fisher Era", JCH VII p. 113.

Paul G. Halpern, *The Mediterranean Naval Situation, 1908-1914* (Cambridge, Massachusetts, 1971).

Sir R. Vesey Hamilton, *Naval Administration* (London, 1869). A thorough, if uncritical, account of the workings of the Admiralty, glancing at its history.
Journals and Letters of Admiral of the Fleet Sir Thomas Byam Martin, 1773-1854 (London, 1894-1902, 3 vols., NRS 24, 12, 19).

Lord Hankey, *The Supreme Command, 1914-1918* (London, 1961, 2 vols.).

Geoffrey Holmes, *British Politics in the Age of Queen Anne* (London, 1967).

Henry Horwitz, *Revolution Politicks: The Career of Daniel Finch, Second Earl of Nottingham, 1647-1730* (Cambridge, 1968).

Richard Hough, *First Sea Lord* (London, 1969). A life of Fisher.

Michael Howard, *The Central Organisation of Defence* (London, 1970). Has a masterly summary of the origins and creation of the Ministry of Defence.

H. C. Hoy, *40 O.B.* (London, 1932). A lightweight history, by Admiral Hall's private secretary.

Edward Hughes, "Civil Service Reform, 1853-5", PA XXXII p. 17 (also *History* XXVII).

Marian Jack. "The Purchase of the British Government's Shares in the British Petroleum Company, 1912-1914", P&P XXXIX p. 139.

G. F. James, "The Admiralty Establishment, 1759", BIHR XVI p. 24.
"Some Further Aspects of Admiralty Administration, 1689-1714", BIHR XVII p. 13.
"Josiah Burchett, Secretary to the Lords Commissioners of the Admiralty, 1695-1742", MM XXIII p. 477.

G. F. James and J. J. S. Shaw, "Admiralty Administration and Personnel, 1619-1714", BIHR XIV pp. 10 and 166. These four studies are of great importance for the administrative development of the Admiralty.

Sir William James, *The Eyes of the Navy* (London, 1955). A life of Sir Reginald Hall.
A Great Seaman (London, 1956). A life of Sir Henry Oliver.

L. J. Jennings (ed.), *The Croker Papers* (London, 1884, 3 vols.).

A. W. Johns, "The Principal Officers of the Navy", MM XIV p. 32.

F. A. Johnson, *Defence by Committee* (London, 1960). This remains a very useful study of the Committee of Imperial Defence, although written before the release of the official documents.

Neville Jones, *The Origins of Strategic Bombing* (London, 1973). The R.N.A.S. had a great deal to do with this.

Gerald Jordan (ed.), *Naval Warfare in the Twentieth Century* (London, 1977).

P. K. Kemp, *The Papers of Admiral Sir John Fisher* (London, 1960-4, 2 vols., NRS 102 and 106).

D. E. Kennedy, "The Establishment and Settlement of Parliament's Admiralty, 1642-8", MM XLVIII p. 276.
"The English Naval Revolt of 1648", EHR LXXVII p. 247.

Stephen King-Hall, *My Naval Life 1906-1929* (London, 1952). Vastly more entertaining, and in places informative, than the usual run of memoirs.

R. J. B. Knight, "Sandwich, Middleton and Dockyard Appointments", MM LVII p. 175.

Robert Latham and William Matthews (eds.), *The Diary of Samuel Pepys* (London, 1970ff, 11 vols.).

Sir J. K. Laughton, *Letters and Papers of Charles, Lord Barham, 1758-1813* (London, 1906-1910, 3 vols., NRS 32, 38, 39). Very important for the developments of naval administration.

Ronald Lewin, *Churchill as Warlord* (London, 1973).

C. C. Lloyd, *Mr. Barrow of the Admiralty* (London, 1970).

Hugh Lyon, "The Relations between the Admiralty and Private Industry in the Development of Warships", in *Technical Change and British Naval Policy, 1860-1939* ex. B. McL. Ranft.

Ruddock F. Mackay, *Admiral Hawke* (Oxford, 1965).
Fisher of Kilverstone (Oxford, 1973).

P. G. Mackesy, *The War for America, 1775-83* (London, 1964). Much more than a study of the war, this masterful and compelling work deals with the structure of politics, administration and society.

G. Marcus, *A Naval History of England: I, The Formative Centuries; II, The Age of Nelson* (London, 1961 and 1971). A general history, best on the eighteenth century.

A. J. Marder, *The Anatomy of British Sea Power* (New York, 1940; Hamden, Connecticut, 1964) *alias: British Naval Policy 1880-1905* (London, 1940).
From the Dreadnought to Scapa Flow (London, 1961-70, 5 vols.). A massive and detailed history of the Navy 1904-20.
Fear God and Dread Nought (London, 1952-59, 3 vols.). The private correspondence of Sir John Fisher.

Sir Clements R. Markham, *The Correspondence of Admiral John Markham, 1801-7*. A member of Barham's Board.

R. G. Marsden (ed.), *Select Pleas in the Court of Admiralty* (London, Selden Society, 1894-7, 2 vols.).

George Martelli, *Jemmy Twitcher; A Life of the Fourth Earl of Sandwich, 1718-1792* (London, 1962).

A. P. McGowan (ed.), *The Jacobean Commissions of Enquiry: 1608 and 1618* (London, 1971, NRS 116). The origin of the first Board of Admiralty.

Donald McLachlan, *Room 39* (London, 1968). Naval Intelligence in the Second World War.

R. D. Merriman (ed.), *The Sergison Papers* (*1688-1702*) (London, 1949, NRS 89). A Clerk of the Acts in the Navy Board.
Queen Anne's Navy (London, 1861, NRS 103).

Richard Middleton, "Pitt, Anson and the Admiralty, 1756-1761", *History*, LV p. 189.

Sir Oswyn A. R. Murray, "The Admiralty, Parts I-X", MM XXIII pp. 13, 129, 316; XXIV pp. 101, 204, 329, 458; XXV p. 89, 216, 328. The greatest of modern Secretaries of the Admiralty was commissioned to write the volume on the Admiralty in the "Whitehall" series, but found that his historical account had overwhelmed what the publisher intended for an administrative study, and abandoned the work unfinished. After his death it was published in parts in *The Mariner's Mirror*.

Lady O. A. R. Murray, *The Making of a Civil Servant* (London, 1940). A life of Murray by his widow.

Peter Nailor, "The Military Bureaucracy: A Case Study of a Civilian Contribution", in *War in the Next Decade* ed. R. Beaumont and M. Edmonds (London, 1975). Civilians and naval officers in the Admiralty.

L. B. Namier, *The Structure of Politics at the Accession of George III* (London, 2nd ed., 1957).

D. Nicholas, *Mr Secretary Nicholas* (London, 1955). The first Secretary of the Admiralty.

M. Oppenheim, *History of the Administration of the Royal Navy and of Merchant Shipping in Relation to the Navy, 1509-1660* (London, 1896). A comprehensive and detailed work, based on extensive research, but his judgement is not always to be relied on, and an alarmingly high proportion of the references are erroneous. *The Naval Tracts of Sir William Monson* (London, 1902-1914, 5 vols., NRS 22, 23, 43, 45, 47). Writing in retirement in James I's reign, Monson reflected on the history and constitution of the Navy in his time.

S. W. C. Pack, *Admiral Lord Anson* (London, 1960).

Henry Parris, *Constitutional Bureaucracy: The Development of British Central Administration since the Eighteenth Century* (London, 1969).

Ann Parry, *Parry of the Arctic* (London, 1936). Not only a famous Arctic explorer, but successively Hydrographer, Comptroller of the Packet Service, and first Inspector of Steam Machinery.

J. H. Parry, *The Age of Reconnaissance* (London, 1963).

A. Temple Patterson (ed.), *The Jellicoe Papers* (London, 1966-8, 2 vols., NRS 108, 111).

G. Penn, *Memorials of the Professional Life and Times of Sir William Penn* (London, 1833, 2 vols.). A distinguished sea commander during the Interregnum, and naval administrator in Charles II's reign.

Samuel Pepys, *Memoires Relating to the State of the Royal Navy of England, for Ten Years Determin'd December 1688* (London, 1690) ed. J. Tanner (Oxford, 1906). Pepys's defence of his tenure of office.

W. G. Perrin, "The Lord High Admiral and the Board of Admiralty", MM XII p. 117. Notes for Lectures on Naval Administration (MS, *ca.* 1929, copy in the author's possession). These notes were complied from materials in the Admiralty Library, of which Perrin was Librarian.

I. Lloyd Phillips, "Lord Barham at the Admiralty, 1805-6", MM XLIV p. 217.

Bernard Pool, *Navy Board Contracts, 1660-1832* (London, 1966).
"Navy Contracts in the Last Years of the Navy Board, 1780-1832", MM L p. 209.

Sir F. M. Powicke and E. B. Fryde (eds.), *Handbook of British Chronology* (London, Royal Historical Society, 2nd ed. 1961). Includes lists of Lords Admiral and First Lords.

W. R. Powell, "The Administration of the Navy and the Stannaries, 1189-1216", EHR LXXI p. 177.

Edward B. Powley, *The English Navy in the Revolution of 1688* (Cambridge, 1928).

Menna Prestwich, *Cranfield: Politics and Profits under the Early Stuarts* (Oxford, 1967). Important member of, and influence on the first Admiralty Board.

R. B. Pugh, "The Early History of the Admiralty Record Office" in *Studies Presented to Sir Hilary Jenkinson* (London, 1957) ed. J. C. Davis.

B. McL. Ranft (ed.), *Technical Change and British Naval Policy, 1860-1939* (London, 1977).

"The Protection of British Seaborne Trade and the Development of Systematic Planning for War, 1860-1906", in *Ibid.*

B. McL. Ranft, "The Significance of the Political Career of Samuel Pepys", JMH XXIV p. 368.

T. F. Reddaway, "Sir Christopher Wren's Navy Office", BIHR XXX p. 175.

H. W. Richmond (ed.), *Papers relating to the Loss of Minorca in 1756* (London, 1911, NRS 42).

The Private Papers of George, second Earl Spencer (London, 1923-4, NRS 58 & 59). The continuation of Vols. I and II ed. Corbett, q.v.

G. S. Ritchie, *The Admiralty Chart—British Hydrography in the Nineteenth Century* (London, 1967).

Gregory Robinson, "Admiralty and Naval Affairs, May 1660 to March 1674", MM XXXVI p. 12.

N. A. M. Rodger, "The Design of the *Inconstant*", MM LXI p.9.

"The Dark Ages of the Admiralty, 1869-85; Pt. I. "Business Methods", 1869-74, Pt. II, "Change and Decay, 1874-80", Pt. III, "Peace, Retrenchment and Reform, 1880-5", MM LXI p. 331, LXII pp. 33 and 121.

"British Belted Cruisers", MM LXIII p. 23. Deal with the methods and personalities of the Admiralty, 1865-1885.

S. W. Roskill, *Hankey, Man of Secrets* (London, 1970-1974, 3 vols.).

Documents Relating to the Naval Air Service, Vol. I, 1908-1918 (London, 1969, NRS 113).

Naval Policy Between the Wars (London, 1968-76, 2 vols.).

Churchill and the Admirals (London, 1977).

All these are masterly and invaluable, especially the last two.

Violet A. Rowe, *Sir Henry Vane the younger* (London, 1970).

J. C. Sainty (ed.), *Admiralty Officials, 1660-1870* (London, Institute of Historical Research, 1975; No. IV of "Office Holders in Modern Britain"). Essential not only for its lists of officials but for the introductions giving the history of each post.

D. M. Schurman, *The Education of a Navy* (London, 1965).

David Bonner Smith (ed.), *The Letters of Lord St. Vincent, 1801-1804* (London, 1921-6, NRS 55 and 61).

"The Admiralty Building", MM IX p. 271.

"The Abolition of the Navy Board", MM XXXI p. 154.

W. P. Snyder, *The Politics of British Defence Policy, 1945-1962* (London, 1964).

Jack Sweetman, "Coronel: Anatomy of a Disaster", in *Naval Warfare in the Twentieth Century* (London, 1977), ed. G. Jordan.

David Syrett, *Shipping and the American War 1775-83* (London, 1970). Wider in scope and more important than its title implies.

J. R. Tanner, *Samuel Pepys and the Royal Navy* (Cambridge, 1920).

Hollond's Discourses of the Navy, 1683 and 1658 (London, 1896, NRS 7).

A Descriptive Catalogue of the Naval MSS in the Pepysian Library (London, 1903-22, 4 vols., NRS 26, 27, 36, 57).

Samuel Pepys's Naval Minutes (London, 1925, NRS 60). The significance of Pepys scarcely needs to be pointed.

A. W. Tedder, *The Navy of the Restoration* (Cambridge, 1916).

Harold Temperley, "A Note on Inner and Outer Cabinets; their Development and Relations in the Eighteenth Century", EHR XXXI p. 291.

M. A. Thomson, *The Secretaries of State, 1681-1782* (Oxford, 1932).

Geoffrey Till, "Airpower and the Battleship" in *Technical Change and British Naval Policy, 1860-1939* (London, 1977) ed. B. McL. Ranft.

W. C. B. Tunstall, "Imperial Defence 1815-1870" in Vol. II of the *Cambridge History of the British Empire* (Cambridge, 1929-63).

The Byng Papers (London, 1930-33, 3 vols., NRS 67, 68, 70).

V. Vale, "Clarendon, Coventry and the Sale of Naval Offices, 1660-1668", CHJ XII p. 107.

Sir Charles Walker, *Thirty-Six Years at the Admiralty* (London, 1933).

J. T. Ward, *Sir James Graham* (London, 1967).

Oliver Warner, *Cunningham of Hyndhope* (London, 1967).

Anthony Wells, "Naval Intelligence and Decision Making in an Age of Technical Change", in *Technical Change and British Naval Policy, 1860-1939* (London, 1977), ed. B. McL. Ranft.

Lady Wemyss, *The Life and Letters of Lord Wester Wemyss* (London, 1935).

F. B. Wickwire, "Kings Friends, Civil Servants or Politicians", AHR LXXI p. 18.

"Admiralty Secretaries and the British Civil Service", HLQ XXVIII p. 235.

Glyndwr Williams (ed.), *Documents relating to Anson's Voyage round the World, 1740-1744* (London, 1967, NRS 109).

J. A. Williamson, *Sir John Hawkins, The Times and the Man* (Oxford, 1927).

Maurice Wright, *Treasury Control of the Civil Service, 1854-1874* (Oxford, 1969).

Index